THE KEYS TO THE CAR:

Electric and

Hydrogen

Vehicles

for the

21st Century

James J. MacKenzie

WORLD
RESOURCES
INSTITUTE

May 1994

Kathleen Courrier
Publications Director

Brooks Belford
Marketing Manager

Hyacinth Billings
Production Manager

Marcie Wolf-Hubbard
Cover Design

Each World Resources Institute Report represents a timely, scholarly treatment of a subject of public concern. WRI takes responsibility for choosing the study topics and guaranteeing its authors and researchers freedom of inquiry. It also solicits and responds to the guidance of advisory panels and expert reviewers. Unless otherwise stated, however, all the interpretation and findings set forth in WRI publications are those of the authors.

CONTENTS

FOREWORD

America's long romance with the internal combustion engine has reached mythic proportions. Between 1970 and 1990, the U.S. automobile population grew almost three times faster than the human one did, and the total distance driven a year doubled. The two trillion miles that Americans now drive every year create smog and acid rain and add 1.1 billion metric tons of carbon dioxide to the atmosphere, accelerating the risk of global climate change. The economic side-effects of our petroleum-based transport system loom over us too: trade imbalances and defense worries grow alongside our appetite for imported oil, which cost $60 billion in 1990 but is projected to top $200 billion by 2010.

Must we sacrifice the mobility and convenience our society has come to expect to end our dependence on the internal combustion engine? No, according to James J. MacKenzie, senior associate in WRI's Climate, Energy, and Pollution program. MacKenzie argues that there is an alternative in the commercial development and widespread use of zero-emission vehicles—which, for now, means electric cars, trucks, and buses.

In *The Keys to the Car: Electric and Hydrogen Vehicles for the 21st Century*, MacKenzie surveys the environmental and economic costs and benefits of alternative fuels, finding that ethanol, methanol, and natural gas can serve, at best, as transitional options. These carbon-based fuels may make the air a bit cleaner here and there, but as they are now produced, they will neither reduce carbon-dioxide emissions enough to slow global climate change nor shrink fuel imports. Electric vehicles will do better. With their use, air pollution would be cut drastically and, if fueled by electricity from natural gas plants or the current mix of electric power plants in the United States, these vehicles would emit only half as much carbon dioxide as gasoline-fueled alternatives. Emissions would fall to zero if the electricity came from photovoltaic, wind, or other renewable energy technologies. Since the nation's electric power grid is fueled by domestic resources, electric vehicles can also help hold the line on fossil fuel imports.

MacKenzie explores the status of electric vehicle research and technology—including batteries, flywheels, ultracapacitors, and hydrogen fuel cells—in the United States, Japan, and Europe. For the next decade or so, most electric vehicles will run on one battery or another, but ultimately they will be powered by some combination of these technologies. To highlight how vital technological advances will be to U.S. automakers' international competitiveness, MacKenzie notes that Japan intends to have 200,000 electric vehicles on the road by 2000 and to build 100,000 of them a year from then on. In France, mass production of electric vehicles will begin in 1995.

To move electric vehicles toward the marketplace in the United States, MacKenzie recommends the following policy shifts:

- *Reforming Fuel Prices.* Raising fuel taxes so that prices reflect the full costs of air pollution, climate change, oil imports, and noise that gasoline-powered cars impose on society is the most important action we can take. To cover these costs, the price of gasoline would have to rise by at least $0.50 a gallon. If it did, electric vehicles with advanced batteries would become cost-competitive with gasoline-powered ones.
- *Shared-Cost Research and Development.* More research and development is needed on batteries and hydrogen technology. Government should share the cost of developing batteries, fuel cells, and hydrogen-storage systems to increase vehicle range (as well as the odds that some electric vehicle technologies will become commercially viable).
- *Infrastructure Development.* Electric vehicles will need a network of standardized recharging facilities, hydrogen-production and -delivery systems, battery-recycling centers, and other equipment. More support on systems-integration

and optimization is needed to determine how vehicles should be refueled and how hydrogen should be produced, transmitted, and stored. Especially important is research on how best to use renewable energy sources to supply electricity and hydrogen in the next century. As standards emerge from these inquiries, building codes should be revamped to make new buildings "electric-vehicle compatible."

- *Stimulating the Market.* Incentives and demonstration programs should be fully implemented to stimulate the market for battery and hydrogen electric vehicles. If such incentives boosted sales to 100,000 a year, the market would become robust, and technical advances and lower prices could be expected. Several recent federal laws, including the Clean Air Act Amendments of 1990, support fleet purchases in states where clean-air standards are violated. These programs should focus mainly on electric vehicles rather than on those powered by methanol, ethanol, or natural gas. Other measures are proposed to encourage the EV market, such as "feebates" to reduce the purchase price of electric vehicles and preferential treatment of these vehicles in such matters as toll road fees, restricted-access lanes, parking, taxes, and registration fees.

The Keys to the Car extends the analyses and recommendations that MacKenzie put forth in the rest of his transportation trilogy, *The Going Rate: What It Really Costs to Drive* and *Driving Forces: Motor Vehicle Trends and Their Implications for Global Warming, Energy Strategies, and Transportation Planning.* He is also co-author of *Car Trouble*, a popular paperback book that explains to a larger audience how new technologies, clean fuels, and creative thinking can revive the U.S. auto industry and reduce pollution and gridlock. MacKenzie's ongoing research on transportation is part of WRI's overall effort to stimulate sustainable development.

We would like to thank The Nathan Cummings Foundation and the W. Alton Jones Foundation, Inc., for their generous financial support of WRI's work on transportation. We also want to express our thanks to The Energy Foundation, The William Penn Foundation, The Joyce Foundation, the Joyce Mertz-Gilmore Foundation, Rockefeller Brothers Fund, and the Public Welfare

Foundation, Inc., for the broad support they have provided to WRI's Climate, Energy, and Pollution program. To all of these institutions, we owe a debt of gratitude.

Jonathan Lash
President
World Resources Institute

ACKNOWLEDGMENTS

This book has benefited especially from the efforts of two: Roger Dower, who read all of the drafts and provided many valuable suggestions for improving it, and Marcia Zalbowitz, whose indefatigable research efforts helped me enormously.

Helpful comments were received from many reviewers, including from within WRI Walt Reid, Allen Hammond, Daryl Ditz, and Keith Kozloff. Outside reviewers include Stan Bull, Kateri Callahan, Mark DeLuchi, Reid Detchon, Jay Harris, Roberta Nichols, David Pimentel, Fereidoon Sioshansi, Dan Sperling, and Ellen Young. While not all the reviewers necessarily agree with all of the conclusions and recommendations put forth here, all of their comments and suggestions were constructive and helpful. Ultimately, of course, the author alone is responsible for the accuracy and recommendations of the report.

Special thanks go to Kathleen Courrier for her skillful editing of the book, to Hyacinth Billings for production management, to Marcie Wolf-Hubbard for creating the book's cover, to Sue Terry for locating many books and reports, and to Eva Vasiliades and Erin Seper for their day-to-day support while the book was in preparation.

I also wish to thank Gus Speth, President of WRI when this research was begun, and Jonathan Lash, the Institute's current president, for their support and encouragement in undertaking this work.

J.J.M.

I.
INTRODUCTION

Over the past century, petroleum-powered motor vehicles have revolutionized how and where countless millions of Americans live, work, and travel. Affordable motor vehicles and cheap gasoline have brought American car owners freedoms and opportunities that were scarcely imaginable just 50 years ago and that citizens in few other countries can even hope to match. As the truck fleet expanded, industry moved goods more quickly and conveniently to markets than ever before. As mass production brought motorized vehicles within reach of the great majority, populations followed new roads from the industrialized cities common at the turn of the century to the sprawling, low-density, suburban residential and commercial developments in which most Americans now live.

For years, Congress and various administrations have grappled with the problems spawned by the rapid growth in motor vehicle use. Yet, success has been elusive. Tailpipe limits on pollution and fuel-efficiency requirements on new cars and light trucks have made new vehicles far less polluting and far more fuel-efficient, but the problems these programs were created to address persist.

Responding anew to the linked problems of urban air pollution, increasing dependence on imported oil, and global warming, the federal government and some states are now encouraging the introduction of alternative fuels for cars, trucks, and other motor vehicles. High on their list are three carbon-based fuels—methanol, compressed natural gas, and ethanol (blended with gasoline)—along with electricity (for instance, batteries) and hydrogen.[a]

---

[a] Electricity and hydrogen are created using primary forms of energy such as fossil fuels. As a result, they are often described as "energy carriers" rather than fuels.

1

A hard look at the arguments for and against the three carbon-based fuels (see the following section) reveals that the United States would receive only marginal benefits from their use, at least as they are now produced. If they were derived from biomass, their impacts on global warming would be more favorable, but only if they could be produced sustainably—a big *if* since major environmental uncertainties remain to be resolved.

For electric vehicles (EVs), the prognosis is much brighter. Indeed, right now EVs powered by some combination of batteries, hydrogen fuel-cells, flywheels, and ultracapacitors are the most promising long-term means of reducing vehicular pollution, carbon dioxide emissions, and the national security risks of importing oil. The purpose of this report is to explore the potential impacts of switching to EVs. What is the present status of EV and hydrogen technologies? How do EV costs compare with those of conventional vehicles? What are the comparative advantages and disadvantages of EVs relative to the alternatives? And by when, and how much, could they help reduce air pollution, carbon-dioxide emissions, and oil imports?

This report addresses these questions and provides policy guidance on how to accelerate the introduction of electric vehicles.

Box 1. How Far Can Alternatively-Fueled Vehicles Take Us?

Although the use of alternative fuels might shrink the various risks posed by motor vehicles, the shift would have no impact on traffic congestion or the transformation of ever more lands to roads and parking lots. Regardless of what is done to usher in cleaner fuels, some combination of higher fuel taxes, road tolls, reductions in parking subsidies to commuters, innovative personal rapid transit (PRT) systems, and more progressive land-use and transportation planning will likely be needed to ease these growing ills.[1] Important as they are, land-use related problems are beyond the scope of this report.

1. MacKenzie, J. et al. *The Going Rate: What it Really Costs to Drive.* World Resources Institute, Washington, D.C., 1992.

Several conclusions emerge forcefully from the overall analysis. First, fuels are not all created equal; in fact, they differ significantly in their resource and environmental ramifications. Second, the United States would be foolish to spend large sums developing fuels, the infrastructure needed to distribute them, and the vehicles to use them if the chosen fuels would not fit into an emissionless and sustainable transportation system. And third, EVs do in fact meet the challenges of providing clean, sustainable transportation for the 21st century.

The Social Impacts of Oil-Powered Vehicles

Motor vehicles, which helped define American culture and the U.S. economy, are also at the heart of several of the country's most pressing problems. Urban air pollution, acid rain, greenhouse gas emissions, growing dependency on insecure foreign oil sources, and a large trade deficit—all stem in part from burning petroleum to power motor vehicles.

Air Pollution

· Burning oil in internal combustion engines releases air pollutants—including carbon monoxide (CO), volatile organic compounds (VOCs), and nitrogen oxides (NO_x)—that contribute to smog. Despite twenty-five years of federal regulation, billions of dollars spent on emission-control devices, and real progress in making new cars "cleaner," motor vehicles remain significant sources of air pollution, particularly carbon monoxide and ozone.[1] By EPA estimates, motor vehicles account for 50 percent of all CO emissions in this country, 29 percent of NO_x emissions, and 27 percent of VOC emissions.[2] *(See Figure 1.)* Some other government authorities maintain that motor vehicles contribute at least half of the VOC and NO_x emissions during the ozone season.[3] As the National Academy of Sciences reported in 1991, the role of cars and trucks in smog formation may be far greater than suggested by EPA's published emission estimates since the agency greatly underestimated VOC emissions from motor vehicles.[4]

~ Air pollution controls on new automobiles began in model year 1968 when VOC and CO emissions from new vehicles were cut by

3

Figure 1. Motor Vehicle Contribution to U.S. Air Pollution Emissions (1990)

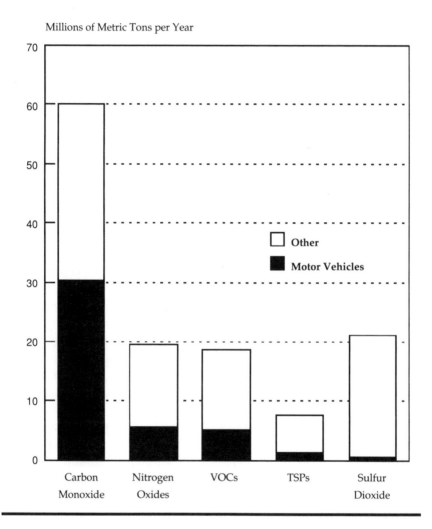

Millions of Metric Tons per Year

about 60 percent. Gradually, controls were strengthened, and by 1992 they reached about 96 percent. Controls of NO_x emissions began in model year 1972. By 1992, NO_x emissions from new cars had been cut by 76 percent.

Despite these dramatic reductions in new-vehicle emissions, in absolute terms, VOC emissions from motor vehicles—as estimated by EPA—fell by only 44 percent over the past two decades and carbon monoxide emissions by only half. And as of late 1991, EPA reports, some 140 million people live in areas where the ozone standard is exceeded.[5]

Behind this public health failure are relentless growth in both the number of motor vehicles and in the human population and the deterioration of the emissions performance of a relatively small percentage of the fleet.[a] Between 1970 and 1990, the U.S. population increased by 23 percent while the number of motor vehicles on the road rose from 108 million to 189 million—a 75 percent jump. By 1990, there were emissions from many more vehicles to contend with—a problem compounded by increasing traffic congestion—and more men, women, and children were exposed to these emissions.

Excessive emissions from a small fraction of older vehicles have also confounded attempts to safeguard air quality. Studies by Douglas Lawson and colleagues suggest that over half of all tailpipe pollution from vehicles comes from only 10 percent of the fleet.[6] *(See Figure 2.)* Yet, many of these high polluters had recently passed state-administered inspection and maintenance tests.

Fleet growth and vehicle deterioration underscore the difficulties of trying to cut pollution by applying "tailpipe fixes"—emission devices and periodic inspections—to conventional cars and trucks. On this path, growth in the vehicle fleet dictates continual technological improvements to cut emissions and better inspection and maintenance programs (supplemented with the use of remote sensors on roadways to identify heavy polluters between inspections) to catch the relatively few high-emission vehicles that can offset hard-bought gains achieved in the rest of the fleet.

Increasing Dependence on Imported Oil

U.S. domestic crude oil production continues its long-term downward decline. *(See Figure 3.)* The production of crude oil in

---

[a] On average, internal combustion engine vehicles emit hydrocarbons at three times the rate to which they were certified—offsetting some of the anticipated clean-air benefits.

5

Figure 2. Average Tailpipe Hydrocarbon Emissions

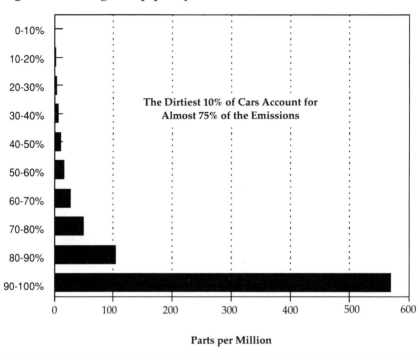

the lower-48 states has fallen 41 percent since its peak in 1970. In Alaska, crude oil output topped out in 1988 and fell by 15 percent over the next four years. The U.S. Department of Energy (DOE) expects U.S. crude oil production to continue its downward slide. In the background analysis prepared for the National Energy Strategy (NES), DOE projected that if current trends continue, domestic crude oil production will fall 34 percent below 1990 levels by 2015 and 64 percent below 1990 levels by 2030.[7] Meanwhile, DOE estimates, domestic oil consumption will continue to grow, increasing by 50 percent over the next forty years. According to DOE's *Annual Energy Outlook* (1994), *net* oil imports could rise from 41 percent of supply in 1992 to between 60 and 75 percent by the year 2010,[8] exacerbating the nation's balance-of-payments

Figure 3. History of U.S. Crude Oil Production

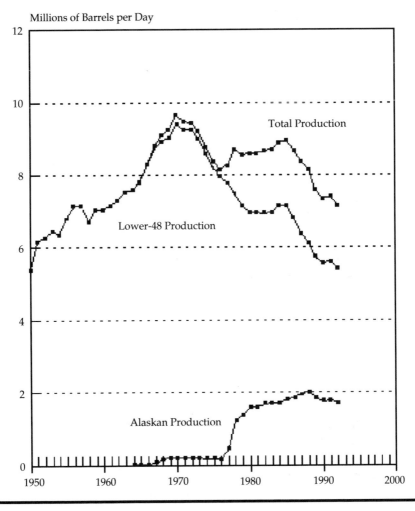

problem and jeopardizing national security. Experts outside the agency concur.[9]

Motor vehicles account largely for the nation's deteriorating oil position. In 1992, cars, trucks, and buses swallowed on average 8.9 million barrels of oil per day, accounting for over half the nation's total oil use.[10] Motor-fuel consumption increased by 19 percent between 1973 and 1992, even though total national demand for oil held steady. (During these two decades, residential and commercial buildings, electric utilities, and industry all cut their oil use substantially.) In short, most of the country's growing oil demand traces back to the transportation sector generally and to motor vehicles specifically.

As petroleum demand grew and production declined over the past decade, oil imports rose. *(See Figures 4 and 5.)* As Figure 4 shows, U.S. oil demand dipped slightly after the 1973 embargo and then more substantially after the 1979 oil shock.[11] The precipitous drop in U.S. oil consumption between 1978 and 1983 (about 21 percent) resulted from skyrocketing oil prices: average crude prices nearly tripled from about $12 per barrel in 1978 to $35 in 1981 and were still almost $29 per barrel in 1983 (all prices in current dollars). Between 1978 and 1983, oil use by utilities dropped by 61 per-

Figure 4. Trends in U.S. Oil Supply

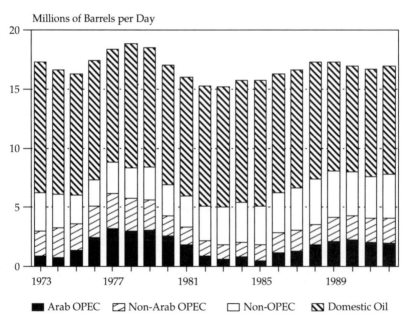

cent; by industry, by 25 percent; and in buildings, by 39 percent. Transportation fuel use fell by only 7 percent.

With this rapid decline in oil demand came a corresponding drop in imports, from 8 million barrels per day (b/d) in 1978 to only 4.31 million b/d in 1983. *(See Figure 5.)* As world oil prices began to soften in the mid-1980s, however, U.S. oil demand swelled again. Between 1985 and 1992, U.S. oil consumption rose by 8 percent and transportation accounted for over 90 percent of the increase.[12] Oil consumption in the transportation sector, dominated by motor vehicles, increased by 22 percent between 1973 and 1992, offsetting general gains. *(See Figure 6.)*

In absolute terms, *net* oil imports (U.S. imports minus U.S. exports) rose by about 60 percent between 1983 and 1992, to about 40 percent of supply. During this period, imports from the Persian Gulf rose from 4 percent of supply to over 12 percent—a trend des-

Figure 5. U.S. Oil Imports (Net)

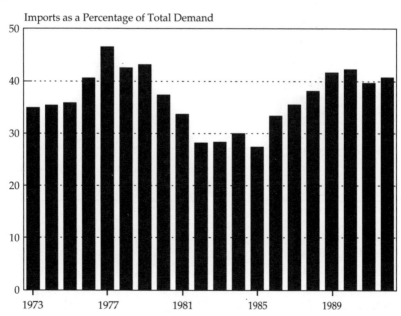

Figure 6. Changes in U.S. Oil Consumption (1973–1992)

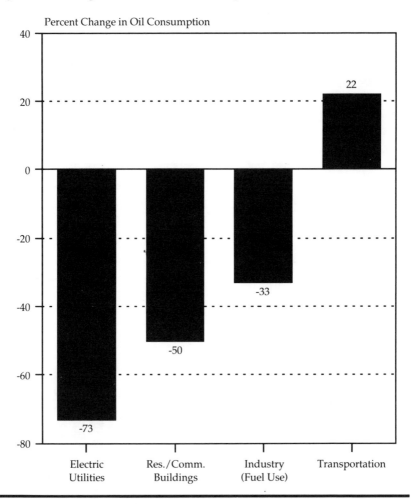

tined to continue, according to the *National Energy Strategy* published in early 1991.[13] *(See Figure 7.)* With increasing reliance on imported oil will come greater threats to U.S. security from potential interruptions in supply and growing balance-of-trade burdens. If the NES estimates are correct, the U.S. bill for imported oil could grow by an average 6.7 percent per year, rising from $60 billion in 1990 to more than $200 billion (in 1990 dollars) by 2010.[14]

Carbon Dioxide Emissions and Global Warming

The so-called greenhouse effect occurs because certain gases in the atmosphere—principally water vapor, carbon dioxide, and methane—allow sunlight to penetrate to the earth, but partially trap the earth's radiated infrared heat. As schoolchildren learn, some greenhouse warming is natural and necessary: without it, the earth would be about 60°F (33°C) colder and life as we know it would not be possible. But over the past two centuries, and especially since 1950 or so, human activities have increased the atmospheric concentrations of the naturally occurring greenhouse gases and added new and powerful artificial infrared-absorbing gases to the mixture. The scientific consensus is strong: if current emission trends continue, basically doubling atmospheric CO_2 concentra-

Figure 7. Global Oil Consumption and Reserves (1992)

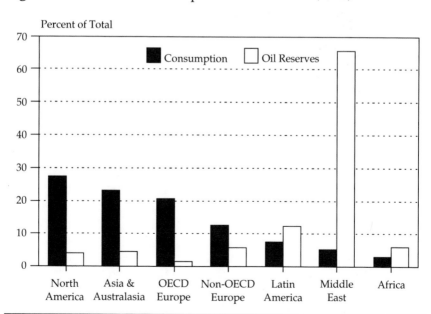

11

tions sometime near the middle of the next century, the earth will respond by warming between 1.5° and 4.5°C.[15] (For perspective here, the temperature rise that took the earth from the depths of the last ice age to the present "interglacial" was only 5°C.)

Uncertainties plague efforts to predict the extent and timing of the regional impacts of global warming. But they could be extensive and last for centuries. Reviewing the potential effects of climate change on the United States, EPA concluded that

> The findings collectively suggest a world different from the world that exists today, although there are many uncertainties about specific effects. Global climate change could have significant implications for natural ecosystems; for where and how we farm; for the availability of water to irrigate crops, produce power, and support shipping; for how we live in our cities; for the wetlands that spawn our fish; for the beaches we use for recreation; and for all levels of government and industry.[16]

Carbon dioxide (CO_2), by far the most important greenhouse gas, is projected to contribute between 67 and 96 percent of the earth's future enhanced warming.[17] According to the Intergovernmental Panel on Climate Change (IPCC), man-made carbon dioxide emissions must be reduced immediately by 60 to 80 percent to stabilize carbon-dioxide concentrations at present levels.[18]

As Figure 8 shows, the transportation sector—including motor vehicles, planes, ships, and pipelines—accounts for almost a third of all CO_2 emissions in the United States. (Only the electric utilities produce more.) Motor vehicles alone account for about 25 percent of total U.S. CO_2 emissions. As Figure 9 shows, CO_2 emissions from motor vehicles have grown steadily over the past three decades, interrupted only by price shocks and recessions. Improvements in motor-vehicle fuel efficiency have been dramatic and the number of miles traveled annually per vehicle has increased only slightly. But the 160-percent increase in the number of motor vehicles on the road—up from 74 million in 1974 to 191 million in 1991—has swamped all progress.

Responding to the oil embargo of 1973, Congress passed the Energy Policy and Conservation Act in 1975, setting up a regulatory framework to increase new-vehicle fuel efficiency. *(See Box 2.)* From 18 miles per gallon (mpg) in 1978, the Corporate Average

Figure 8. Carbon Dioxide Emissions in the U.S. by Sector and Fuels (1992)

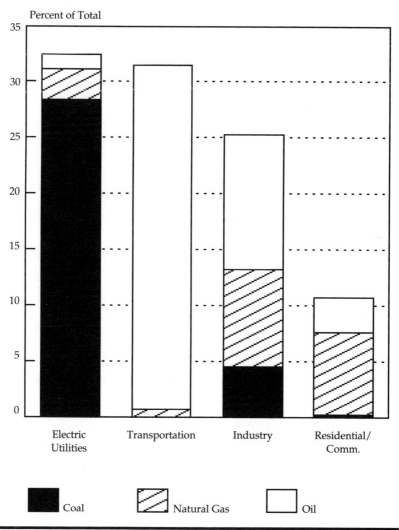

Percent of Total

Coal   Natural Gas   Oil

Fuel Efficiency standard (CAFE, for short) increased year by year to 27.5 mpg in model year 1985. In model years 1986–88, the CAFE requirement was relaxed by the Secretary of Transportation from

13

Figure 9. Annual Carbon Dioxide Emissions from U.S. Motor Vehicles

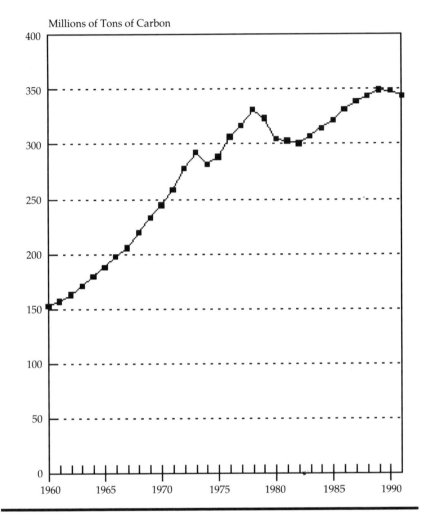

Millions of Tons of Carbon

27.5 mpg to 26 mpg. In model year 1989, it was set at 26.5 mpg, and since 1990 it has been 27.5 mpg.

CAFE standards have only partially succeeded in reducing fuel use (and, therefore, carbon-dioxide emissions). *New-car* fuel effi-

Box 2. Corporate Average Fuel Efficiency (CAFE)
Requirements for New Automobiles (miles per gallon)

	Federal Standard	Domestic Cars	Imported Cars	Total Fleet
1974	None	13.2	22.2	14.2
1975	None	14.8	23.3	15.8
1976	None	16.6	25.4	17.5
1977	None	17.2	27.7	18.3
1978	18.0	18.7	27.3	19.9
1979	19.0	19.3	26.1	20.3
1980	20.0	22.6	29.6	24.3
1981	22.0	24.2	31.5	25.9
1982	24.0	25.0	31.1	26.6
1983	26.0	24.6	32.4	26.4
1984	27.0	25.6	32.0	26.9
1985	27.5	26.3	31.5	27.6
1986	26.0	26.6	31.6	28.2
1987	26.0	27.0	31.2	28.5
1988	26.0	27.4	31.5	28.8
1989	26.5	27.2	30.8	28.4
1990	27.5	26.9	29.8	28.0
1991	27.5	27.4	29.8	28.3
1992	27.5	26.9	29.0	27.8

Source: U.S. Department of Transportation.

ciency increased from 14.2 mpg in 1974 to 28.8 mpg in 1988 as fuel prices and sales of fuel-efficient Japanese vehicles rose and as the CAFE requirements took hold. But between 1988 and 1992, new-car fuel efficiency declined 3.1 percent to 27.9 mpg, largely because gasoline prices sagged to an all-time low. *(See Figure 10.)*

Figure 10. Real Price of Gasoline (in 1993 dollars)

How much the CAFE standards have improved the efficiency of the U.S. auto fleet is still being debated.[19] The average fuel efficiency of the total U.S. passenger-car fleet increased from 13 mpg in 1973 to about 21 mpg in 1990 while the average efficiency of the entire auto-truck fleet increased from 12 mpg in 1973 to about 16 mpg in 1990. But, despite these efficiency gains, U.S. gasoline demand rose 25 percent between 1970 and 1990.[20] Total motor vehicle fuel use—including diesel fuel—increased by more than 40 percent during these years while oil imports more than doubled.[21] One upward push on fuel consumption was the substitution of trucks for cars in daily commuting: between 1980 and 1992, sales of light trucks (including minivans and sport utility vehicles) rose from 20 percent of all light-duty vehicle sales to 36 percent.[22]

Continued growth in motor vehicle use also helped increase national oil consumption (with its attendant increase in CO_2 emissions) and U.S. dependence on imported oil. Over the two decades beginning in 1970, the number of cars on the road grew by 61 percent; the number of licensed drivers, by 50 percent; the use of trucks and vans (which are relatively inefficient), by 278 percent; and the number of miles that the average vehicle was driven, by 11 percent.[23] In short, motor vehicle use grew in virtually every aspect. Oil consumption increases led inevitably to greater emissions of carbon dioxide, the principal greenhouse gas. Indeed, these vehicular emissions—mainly from cars, trucks, and buses—increased along with fuel use by over 40 percent between 1970 and 1991. *(See Figure 9.)* And recent projections suggest that U.S. vehicle-fuel use (and CO_2 emissions) could increase between 5 and 50 percent over 1987 levels by 2010.[24] Worldwide jumps in carbon-dioxide emissions from motor vehicles (20 to 50 percent by 2010) are also plausible.[25]

Federal and State Initiatives for Bringing Alternative Fuels on Line

Since deep cuts in new-car tailpipe emissions and parallel improvements in fuel efficiency have not been enough to realize clean air goals or to offset rising motor-vehicle fuel use, Congress adopted new measures to help reduce pollution and cut oil consumption. Title II of the Clean Air Act Amendments (CAAA) of 1990 (P.L. 101-549) dictates stricter tailpipe emission limits and the sale of cleaner-burning reformulated gasoline in regions where ozone problems are worst.[26] The law also prescribes the oxygen content of motor vehicle fuels and places limits on fuel volatility. The amendments specify that "clean fuel" vehicles—those powered by reformulated gasoline

17

or alternative fuels—must be used in fleets in certain so-called non-attainment areas, and they establish a clean-fuel pilot program in California to introduce ethanol, methanol, compressed natural gas, liquefied petroleum gas (propane), electricity, and other such "alternative fuels" as hydrogen.

Congress has also spoken on motor vehicle fuels in the Energy Policy Act passed in October 1992.[27] Under this law, those who own or operate more than 50 vehicles and who have at least one centrally-fueled fleet of 20 vehicles in an urban area with a population of at least 250,000 must purchase "alternative fueled vehicles" (dedicated or bi-fuel vehicles that run on alternative fuels). The federal government must purchase at least 5,000 of these vehicles in 1993, increasing to 7,500 in 1994 and 10,000 in 1995.[a] By 1996, one fourth of all new federal cars and light trucks have to run on alternative fuels. The percentage reaches 33 percent by 1997, 50 percent in 1998, and 75 percent in 1999 and thereafter. (For reference, if Department of Defense vehicles are included, the federal fleet consists of about 450,000 cars and light trucks.[28])

States are also required to purchase alternative fueled vehicles. Beginning in 1995 (model year 1996), 10 percent of new vehicles must be alternatively fueled. In 2000 and beyond, 75 percent must be. Initially, the only private fleets affected are those owned by companies that produce, transport, store, or sell alternative fuels. For ethanol producers, natural gas distributors, and electric utilities, 30 percent of the new vehicles in 1996 must use alternative fuels, increasing to 90 percent in 1999 and thereafter.[b] The Act also authorizes DOE to impose requirements to purchase alternative fuel vehicles on private companies and local governments, beginning as early as 1999, should DOE find such requirements "necessary and practicable" to achieve the goals of the Act.

The energy bill authorizes DOE to set up joint ventures with industry to demonstrate electric vehicles. It also authorizes contin-

---

[a] On April 21, 1993, President Clinton signed an executive order to increase federal purchases of alternative fueled vehicles by 50 percent over these requirements.

[b] Recognizing the development status of EVs, the law provides a two-year "grace period" from the 1996 compliance deadline for electric utilities that inform the federal government of their intent to comply with the requirements through the use of EVs.

ued and expanded federal R&D efforts on EVs and hybrid vehicles. The law also creates a new program to assist states in developing incentives for alternative fuels and vehicles, and provides tax credits and deductions for purchasing alternative vehicles. Tax deductions range up to $2,000 for cars and up to $50,000 for heavy trucks, and businesses that install refueling stations can take a $100,000 tax deduction. An income tax credit of 10 percent of the electric vehicle's cost is provided, with a maximum of $4,000. The bill also extends to other ethanol-gasoline blends the current 5.4-cent-per-gallon exemption from federal gasoline taxes for gasohol (a blend of 90 percent gasoline and 10 percent ethanol).

States too are promoting alternative fuels. California leads the world in efforts to identify, develop, and introduce low-polluting fuels and transportation systems. In September 1990, the California Air Resources Board (CARB) adopted its Low Emissions Vehicle (LEV) regulations, establishing progressively more stringent car emission standards for VOCs, NO_x, and CO. By 1998, two percent of new cars and light trucks will have to be Zero Emission Vehicles (ZEVs) that give off no VOCs, NO_x, or CO.[29] By 2001, five percent of new cars and light trucks sold in California must be ZEVs; by 2003 and later, 10 percent. The only vehicles expected to meet the CARB requirements any time soon are electric cars and trucks, though hydrogen-powered vehicles using fuel cells could also qualify if they become commercially available. CARB's ZEV regulations have pulled major automobile manufacturers the world over into the race to develop electric and hydrogen-powered vehicles.

To curb air pollution, 12 northeastern states, and the District of Columbia, have publicly committed to following California. (California and these states together account for almost 40 percent of U.S. new-car sales.[30]) As of March 1994, Maine, Massachusetts, Maryland, New Jersey, and New York had adopted California's LEV regulations. In some states, though, U.S. automakers have challenged these actions in federal court. In February 1994, the Second Circuit Court of Appeals upheld New York's adoption of California's LEV regulations including the mandate for production and sale of ZEVs. In February 1994, the Ozone Transport Commission—the air regulators of the 12 northeast states and Washington, D.C.—voted to petition EPA to impose California's LEV regula-

19

tions on the region; and EPA has nine months to approve or disapprove the proposal.

Meanwhile, the fate of California's LEV regulations, a major impetus to international EV efforts, is in some doubt. Lobbying California to change or postpone its requirements to begin introducing EVs in 1998, U.S. automakers argue that battery technology is still too expensive and too immature to appeal to consumers. Although the California Air Resources Board seems determined not to back down,[31] it is legally bound to review feasibility every other year, including 1994.

* * *

⚒ The clear goal of recent federal legislation and state initiatives is to encourage the substitution of alternative fuels for gasoline. But more attention needs to be paid to whether using more of these fuels would significantly improve air quality, forestall climate change, curb energy imports, or enhance national security. Why overhaul the nation's energy infrastructure and make huge financial investments in new fuels unless these alternatives provide clear-cut benefits to justify the effort?

II.

EMERGING VEHICLE TECHNOLOGIES: WEIGHING THE ALTERNATIVES

Five major energy forms (plus reformulated gasoline) are currently being promoted as replacements for gasoline and diesel fuel in motor vehicles: methanol, compressed natural gas (CNG), ethanol, electricity (from batteries), and hydrogen.[32] The U.S. EPA and the State of California, especially the California Energy Commission, have long advocated switching to methanol vehicles to reduce ozone concentrations, particularly in the Los Angeles basin. The desire to improve air quality also underlies the push toward CNG cars, trucks, and buses. Ethanol is being promoted as a domestic energy source, as well as a means of reducing carbon monoxide concentrations. Electric and hydrogen-powered vehicles are being advocated to reduce oil imports and to cut air pollution and greenhouse gas emissions.

As the following comparative analysis shows, alternative fuels do not have the same impacts on global warming, national security, and air quality.[a] The comparisons presented here—based largely on existing technology, which presumably could always be improved—highlight these critical differences.

Methanol

Methanol (properly, methyl alcohol, but also known as wood alcohol) is currently made almost exclusively from natural gas. At

---

[a] Indeed, in many respects the impacts of a "fuel" by itself cannot be determined in any absolute sense. They will depend very much on the processes used to produce the fuel (as in the case of alcohol fuels) and on the emissions-control technologies on the vehicles. With sufficient money and time, vehicles powered by any fuel can be made to run with very low pollution emissions. In this sense, no ultimate ranking of fuels is possible.

a higher cost, it could also be produced from coal, biomass, or almost any carbon-rich material. Under current proposals by both California and the federal government, methanol would be introduced in flexible-fuel vehicles that can burn methanol-gasoline blends ranging from pure gasoline (or M0, for zero percent methanol) to a mixture of 85 percent methanol and 15 percent gasoline (M85). For several reasons, manufacturers are not planning to produce automobiles operating on pure methanol (M100). These vehicles are difficult to start at temperatures below 40° to 50°F, and cars running only on M100 wouldn't have much of a market until a dispersed network of service stations supplying 100-percent pure methanol was built. (To some extent, the use of any "dedicated" vehicle running on just one alternative fuel entails this problem.)

Initially, methanol supporters figured that emissions from methanol vehicles would contribute less than gasoline-related emissions to ozone formation.[33] But would they? According to Sierra Research, Inc. of Sacramento, California, "...the previously assumed [ozone] air quality benefits of methanol-fueled vehicles do not exist."[34] After analyzing both actual emissions and reactivity data from a flexible-fuel vehicle capable of running on gasoline or methanol blends, Sierra engineers concluded that if both gasoline and methanol-fueled vehicles meet the most stringent emission standards yet adopted, methanol-fueled vehicles are projected to form slightly *more* ozone than gasoline-fueled vehicles, not less.[35] The Sierra team believes that its findings cast "doubt on the assumptions underlying the current focus on methanol as a 'clean' alternative fuel for automobiles." Nor do these researchers believe that the relative ozone-forming potentials of gasoline and methanol blends have changed since 1990. According to Sierra engineer Tom Austin "while the emissions from methanol-fueled vehicles are less reactive, methanol-fueled vehicles have inherently higher mass emissions of organic material...[so] the theoretical benefits of the lower reactivity of methanol exhaust are counterbalanced by the higher emission rate."[36]

In December 1991, the National Research Council (NRC) of the National Academy of Sciences released a major report on the nation's ozone problem, the relative roles of VOCs and NO_x in ozone formation, and the potential benefits of methanol and other fuels in reducing ozone exposures.[37] Even if Los Angeles' *entire* light-duty fleet of cars and trucks were replaced by methanol vehicles, it found, peak ozone concentrations would fall by only 4 percent. According to the report, any ozone reductions from a switch to M85 would be modest and would be quite sensitive to the percentages of methanol and gasoline burned in the vehicles:

> If flexibly fueled vehicles are used, air-quality benefits likely will be achieved only if M85 or purer fuel is used consistently. If most vehicles were running on a more dilute blend (say M50 or M25), increased evaporative and other organic emissions could lead to increases in ozone.[38]

The overall air quality impacts of using methanol blends and methanol oxygenates (MTBE) were assessed by a group of academic engineers in July 1993 in *Science* magazine.[39]

> The alcohol fuels, [methanol and ethanol], especially when blended with gasoline and used in flexible fuel vehicles, provide little or no air quality advantages beyond the reduction of CO.

> ...the addition of oxygenates, such as methyl tertiary butyl ether (MTBE) and ethanol, has been found to have little or no effect on the problems of atmospheric reactivity and ozone formation.[40]

Methanol, at least when made from fossil fuels, offers little global warming benefit. According to a Congressional Office of Technology Assessment (OTA) report, methanol "...use is expected to provide, at best, only a small greenhouse gas benefit over gasoline, and then only if the vehicles are significantly more efficient than gasoline vehicles."[41] OTA concludes that even switching to highly efficient flexible-fuel vehicles burning M85 from fossil fuels will do nothing to halt global warming.

After an exhaustive comparison of alternative fuels, Mark DeLuchi of the University of California at Davis reached the same conclusion.[42] Light-duty vehicles running on methanol derived from natural gas would emit about the same amount of greenhouse gases as gasoline vehicles, says DeLuchi, while heavy-duty vehicles running on methanol would emit about 20 percent *more* greenhouse gases than diesel-powered vehicles do. Light-duty vehicles running on methanol made from coal would emit almost 60 percent more greenhouse gases than gasoline-powered vehicles do while heavy-duty vehicles would emit about twice as much greenhouse gases as their oil-powered counterparts. (Producing *any* synthetic fuel from coal results in high carbon dioxide emissions.)

Although inexpensive domestic supplies of natural gas are limited,[43] worldwide, supplies appear adequate, and non-OPEC sources could probably save methanol suppliers from becoming dangerously dependent on Persian Gulf sources. Still, upheaval in the Middle East could destabilize supplies and prices from otherwise "secure" sources. In any case, some imports would be essential and consuming methanol made overseas would not help the nation's balance-of-trade problems.

Compressed Natural Gas (CNG)

Some decision-makers are advocating the use of natural gas, primarily as CNG, to reduce air pollution and reliance on imported oil. Canada, Italy, New Zealand, and a few other countries already use CNG as a motor fuel. Worldwide, some 700,000 CNG vehicles are in service, and experience with its use in fleets is considerable. Although their NO_x emissions are at least as great as those from gasoline-powered vehicles, CNG vehicles emit comparatively little carbon monoxide, reactive hydrocarbons, and particulates.[44] According to OTA and the National Research Council, a switch to CNG vehicles would definitely reduce ozone concentrations, at least in regions where VOC reductions are required.[45]

Two technological barriers keep CNG vehicles off the road. One is the need for bulky gas-storage tanks, especially in automobiles, and the other is the absence of a network of refueling stations. (Fears about safety, on the other hand, have been largely quelled by experience.[46]) Right now, the only dual-fuel CNG-gasoline vehicles that are economically attractive are such heavily used vehicles as taxis.[47] The lower price of natural gas (subject—as of October 1, 1993—to a fuel tax equivalent to 6 cents per gallon of gasoline) is largely offset by the higher costs of building CNG dual-fuel vehicles and filling stations, though the economics could improve if dedicated CNG vehicles were manufactured.

If CNG vehicles were introduced, U.S. gas imports would almost certainly increase, especially from Canada.[48] U.S. natural gas consumption has been rising since 1986 while proved reserves have continued to drop.[49] Gas imports, primarily from Canada, have been growing since 1986 and by 1992 accounted for about 11 percent of total supply.[50] Even if CNG vehicles aren't introduced, all major U.S. gas-supply forecasts project growing gas imports during the 1990s and beyond.[51] While increased imports from Canada would hardly threaten U.S. security, they would still contribute to the country's overall trade deficit.

Per vehicle-mile traveled, CNG cars emit less carbon dioxide than gasoline-powered cars. But methane, the principal component of natural gas, is itself a potent greenhouse gas. On balance, DeLuchi estimates, using CNG vehicles could reduce overall greenhouse gas emissions for light-duty vehicles by 15 percent and increase those of heavy-duty diesel-powered vehicles by about 5 percent.[52]

Because they rely on a fossil fuel and thus emit carbon dioxide, CNG vehicles aren't the answer to our long-term pollution and climate problems. But their limited use in North America (where natural gas is available) would reduce pollution emissions, especially from urban buses and trucks. In this niche, CNG vehicles could make a positive, though ultimately transitional, contribution to reducing the risks of air pollution and energy security. Also, experience with CNG vehicles might make it easier to introduce hydrogen-powered vehicles later since the two technologies are similar.

Ethanol

Ethanol (ethyl alcohol, also known as grain alcohol) is the intoxicating ingredient in alcoholic beverages. In 1991, gasohol (nine parts gasoline and one part ethanol) accounted for about 6 percent of U.S. motor-fuel consumption.[53] Congress and some agricultural states, have promoted the use of ethanol in cars, claiming that it will reduce carbon-monoxide emissions when blended with gasoline.

About 95 percent of the ethanol used in motor vehicles in the United States is derived from corn,[54] and the greatest political support for ethanol comes from corn-growing states. But despite gasohol's political popularity, greater use of this fuel wouldn't significantly reduce ozone levels. Nor would corn-based ethanol appreciably reduce the threat of global warming. In a study of ethanol's impacts on air quality, Sierra Research concluded that gasohol would on average reduce CO concentrations by 25 percent, but would increase NO_x emissions by 8 to 15 percent and evaporative emissions of VOCs by 50 percent.[55] Switching to gasohol, the researchers estimated, would *increase* ozone concentrations by at least 6 percent. The Office of Technology Assessment also concluded that ethanol would not help cut smog concentrations:

> ...recent government studies indicate that future use of ethanol blends, assuming modern vehicles, low volatility gasoline, and no volatility corrections made for blending, will have negligible impact on urban ozone levels....[56]

A review in 1993 of air pollution from motor vehicles also found that switching to ethanol blends won't do much to conquer smog.[57] Indeed, it concluded that the "addition of ethanol to gasoline is generally counterproductive with respect to ozone formation...[and that no] convincing argument based on combustion or atmospheric chemistry can be made for the addition of ethanol to gasoline."

Estimates of the net greenhouse impacts of ethanol are subject to great uncertainty. All depend on which feedstock is used, what fuels are used in distillation, and how much energy is credited to the by-products (such as animal feeds, in the case of corn) of ethanol production. According to OTA, the corn-based technology now used to produce ethanol offers no significant greenhouse benefit. Calculating the greenhouse gas emissions for vehicles running on pure ethanol (E100), DeLuchi concludes that switching to motor vehicles running on E100—made from corn—would increase greenhouse gas emissions by 20 percent (for light-duty vehicles) to 50 percent (for heavy-duty vehicles).[58] DeLuchi also points out, though, that these results reflect a wide range of assumptions about the processes for producing ethanol and that:

> "The general message of the corn-to-ethanol scenarios is that one can pick values for a set of assumptions that will support virtually any conclusion about the impact of the corn-to-ethanol cycle on global warming."[59]

Like CNG, ethanol is subsidized by the federal and some state governments. The federal tax subsidy on gasohol is 5.4 cents per gallon (or $0.54 per gallon of ethanol).[60] Several states also reduce their fuel taxes on gasohol.[61] In 1990, combined federal and state subsidies amounted to $467 million.[62] The average federal/state subsidy in 1990 was about $0.62 per gallon of ethanol, with present production costs estimated at $0.90 to $1.15 per gallon. The subsidy thus amounts to 50 to 70 percent of total production costs.

Producing ethanol from corn requires large amounts of land. To fuel a typical American car for a year on pure ethanol would take about 14 acres of corn—about nine times the amount of cropland needed to feed an average American.[63] Even devoting the nation's entire corn crop, some 8 billion bushels, to ethanol production would displace less than 10 percent of the country's motor vehicle fuel. Moreover, growing corn year after year causes serious erosion. According to a recent OTA report, U.S. corn production erodes about 9 tons of soil per acre per year, some 20 times faster than new soil is formed.[64] For these reasons, replacing all motor fuels with ethanol-from-corn is out of the question, and ethanol proponents agree that corn would not be used for making more than 2-3 billion gallons per year.[65]

Alcohol Fuels from Other Biomass Sources

Ethanol and methanol can be produced from other sources of biomass, whether waste paper, municipal solid waste, agricultural and forestry residues and wastes, or low-grade "junk wood" stands.[66] Fuels made from these agricultural and forest residues and municipal wastes might add up to the equivalent of 20 percent (four quads) of all transportation oil.[67] But the removal of forest and agricultural residues would have to be carefully evaluated since it could reduce soil humus and increase erosion, water runoff, and nutrient loss.[68]

By far the largest potential source of alcohol fuels would be energy plantations, where crops or trees would be grown as a feedstock.[69] Estimates of how much U.S. land could be used to grow energy crops vary widely with assumptions.[70] At the high end, the National Renewable Energy Laboratory (NREL) estimates that 190 million acres could be used to grow energy crops for the production of alcohol fuels.[71] (For perspective, active U.S. cropland totals about 330 million acres.) *If each of these 190 million acres could sustainably yield 9 dry tons of biomass per year, they could produce 26 quads of feedstock annually. If this feedstock were then converted to alcohol at a 50-percent conversion efficiency, the yield would be the equivalent of about 100 billion gallons of gasoline*—approximately three quarters of today's U.S. gasoline and diesel fuel consumption. Under NREL's most optimistic growth scenario (made in 1990), about two quads of ethanol (equivalent in energy to about 12 percent of 1992 U.S. motor fuel consumption) could be produced by 2010 and about twice this amount by 2020.[72]

Biomass energy crops would need to be intensively managed, like agricultural crops,[73] and current research reflects this need. DOE's Oak Ridge National Laboratory has a program to develop low-cost feedstocks for alcohol production, particularly from short-rotation (3 to 8 years) hardwood trees and herbaceous grasses. NREL is developing more-efficient, low-cost processes for converting these cellulosic feedstocks into alcohols. Since converting these forms of biomass to alcohol appears to be considerably more energy-efficient than converting corn,[74] using ethanol derived from these sources could decrease overall greenhouse gas emissions. DeLuchi estimates that under favorable conditions—very energy-efficient processes using little or no fertilizer—total emissions of all greenhouse gases from wood-based ethanol could decline by as much as 75 percent compared with those from gasoline.[75] He also points out, though, that:

> ...if wood plantations require a lot of fertilizer, and if the manufacture of materials and equipment results in substantial emissions of greenhouse gases (and if other unfavorable conditions hold), then the biofuel cycles will provide no more than modest reductions—and perhaps even no reduction at all—in greenhouse gas emissions.[76]

Growing energy crops on a large scale entails some potentially significant environmental problems.[77] For example, growing short-rotation trees can lead to a loss of topsoil and nutrients and to soil compaction and increased water runoff. It can also require heavy applications of fertilizer and herbicide. Soil erosion where trees are harvested every five years has been estimated at two metric tons per hectare per year, while forest soils are formed at only 0.3 metric tons per hectare per year.[78] According to OTA, if no conservation measures are taken when the energy crops are established, erosion rates could match those of corn.[79] Detailed analyses of erosion rates for energy crops have yet to be made, and most existing data are on small field trials collected over short periods.[80] Nevertheless, soil erosion appears to be significantly less severe with herbaceous crops than with trees.

In many parts of the world, especially in developing countries, growing energy crops for motor vehicles could compete with food production at a time when climate change could be straining agricultural production. Many tropical and subtropical countries appear more vulnerable to climate change than temperate countries.[81] Of particular concern are the risks of increased lowland flooding, more frequent and severe droughts in semiarid areas, and decreases in crop yields. Hence, at least in these countries, transportation fuels derived from biomass are unlikely to be a practical option.

Summing Up the Pros and Cons of Carbon-Based Fuels

None of the three carbon-based alternative fuels convincingly solves the wide-ranging problems posed by today's heavy reliance on petroleum-powered cars and trucks. *(See Box 3.)* Substituting methanol or ethanol blends for gasoline could reduce national security risks and carbon-monoxide emissions, but would not necessarily cut smog levels or slow global warming. While using ethanol derived from cellulosic biomass might reduce greenhouse gas emissions, the ethanol-from-corn lobby shows no signs of abandoning its large and growing investment in corn. And while CNG use would reduce both carbon monoxide and smog pollution and cut security risks, this fuel would still be imported (most likely from Canada) and using it would slow greenhouse warming only slightly.

Perhaps the most difficult challenge in the search for alternative fuels is greatly reducing carbon dioxide, methane, and nitrous

Box 3. Comparison of Alternative Fuels

	National Security	Smog	Balance of Trade	Global Warming	Cost
Ethanol*					
Methanol					
Natural Gas					

Shaded boxes indicate No Significant Benefit Over Gasoline
Clear boxes indicate Some Likely Benefit Over Gasoline
*No global warming benefit if made from corn

oxide emissions to combat global warming. For reducing carbon-dioxide emissions, alternatives based on fossil fuels are not the answer. Using biomass as a feedstock for alcohol production would help, but is it feasible and practicable to produce large amounts of carbon-based fuels this way *on a sustainable basis*? Although organic wastes can certainly be used as feedstocks, most experts agree that large-scale energy crops are the most promising source for "growing" fuels, particularly alcohol fuels. At issue are the availability of enough suitable land; the costs, effects, and availability of pesticides, fertilizers, and water; the long-term ecological impacts on soils of frequent harvesting of fast-growing crops; the efficiency and costs of the conversion processes; and climate changes that could affect crop production. Until global warming's effects on agriculture[82] are better understood, the overall practicality of growing crops on a massive scale to fuel motor vehicles cannot be evaluated.

III.

ELECTRIC VEHICLES

If natural gas and the alcohol fuels aren't the ideal options for powering the vehicles of the next century, that still leaves batteries, other electrical storage devices (such as flywheels or ultracapacitors), and hydrogen fuel-cells. Electric vehicles "fueled" by these new technologies are expected to be highly reliable, require little maintenance, and, with the right source of electricity, be almost pollution-free. In addition, their greenhouse-gas emissions are comparatively low. Electric vehicles, however, are not without their drawbacks. Initially, at least, they will have higher price tags and shorter ranges than their gasoline-powered competitors, and battery vehicles could take 15 minutes to 8 hours to recharge—far longer than a routine stop at a gas station. Moreover, producing the electricity or hydrogen that these vehicles require entails various problems.

How much a shift to electrically powered vehicles would cut global warming and air pollution emissions will depend mostly on the electric efficiency of the vehicles (measured, for instance, in kilowatt-hours needed to travel one mile) and the amount of emissions (CO_2, CO, SO_2, VOCs, NO_x) from the power plants that produce the electricity used to charge them. Eventually, carbon-dioxide and air-pollution emissions could be virtually eliminated if vehicles were charged with either renewable power sources (photovoltaic cells, wind machines, and so forth) or nuclear electricity (should nuclear power plants once again become publicly acceptable). In these circumstances, greenhouse gas emissions would be reduced between 95 percent (nuclear electricity) and almost 100 percent (solar electricity).[83] And regardless of which fuel is used to generate the electricity, EVs could be powered strictly from domestic

31

sources—a boon to both national security and the nation's balance of trade.

As Section IV of this report makes clear, converting to electric vehicles would significantly improve urban air quality. EVs emit no tail-pipe pollutants, and if the batteries were recharged at night, so that utilities wouldn't have to add any new capacity, the nation's current and planned power plants would suffice for many years and concentrations of ozone and carbon monoxide would drop dramatically. Charging the vehicles with electricity from coal plants would be expected to *increase* national sulfur-dioxide emissions. But since total national sulfur emissions are capped by the 1990 amendments to the Clean Air Act, they would be the same with or without electric vehicles.

Interest in vehicles powered by hydrogen fuel-cells has increased over the past decade, especially in Japan and Germany. These battery-like devices recombine hydrogen and oxygen, producing only electricity, water, and waste heat. Hydrogen vehicles can also be powered using internal combustion engines: a prototype developed by Mazda has a rotary engine. But a hydrogen fuel-cell vehicle would have at least twice the range of a similar hydrogen vehicle powered by an internal combustion engine.

Most hydrogen today is obtained from natural gas, a depletable source. Production of hydrogen from water—either through electrolysis or direct photochemical reactions—is the most likely long-term source! (The primary energy would be supplied by renewable or nuclear technologies.) In either case, virtually no carbon dioxide or pollution emissions would result.

Although hydrogen-fuel-cell vehicles share many of the attractive features of battery EVs, their widespread commercial use is some distance down the road. Fuel-cell technology is less mature and there is little infrastructure to support its use. Still, like battery-powered vehicles, fuel-cell powered vehicles would take us one step toward developing a sustainable energy system. Their use would cut air pollution and greenhouse gas emissions, reduce oil imports, and mitigate the U.S. trade deficit. Since a national pipeline system might be needed to distribute this fuel widely, the natural gas industry could help engineer the hydrogen economy, eventually providing the transmission and compression facilities and, perhaps, even the hydrogen itself.

A. Battery-Powered Electric Vehicles

By far the most advanced electric vehicles are those powered by batteries. The first prototype battery-powered electric vehicle was constructed by a Scottish inventor, Robert Davidson, in 1837.[84] In 1892, William Morrison of Des Moines, Iowa designed and built America's first four-wheel EV. Morrison's EV required 24 storage battery cells, took ten hours to charge, and could run for 13 hours. It carried 12 people, had a four-horsepower motor, and could reach speeds of 14 miles per hour (mph).[85] Despite immense public interest, Morrison never put his vehicle into mass production. The United States saw its first commercially produced battery-powered EV in 1894—the Electrobat, manufactured by the Morris and Salom Company of Philadelphia.[86]

By the late 1890s, EVs—with a typical range of 50 miles, much like today's—dominated the automobile market.[87] Clean and quiet, they proved especially popular in cities. By 1900, 38 percent of new American automobiles ran on batteries. (Steam-powered cars accounted for 40 percent of the new fleet, and gas-driven cars for 22 percent.[88]) By 1912, some 6,000 electric cars and trucks were

Box 4. What Makes an EV an EV?

An electric vehicle (EV) is powered by motors fed by electricity derived on board from batteries, hydrogen-powered fuel cells, flywheels, ultracapacitors—or some combination of these. Electric vehicles are the only vehicles today that qualify as zero emission vehicles (ZEVs) under California's clean air regulations. (Water vapor from a fuel cell is not considered a pollutant.) If the vehicle's electrical power is derived totally or partially from an on-board fuel-burning engine and generator, the vehicle is considered a hybrid.

manufactured each year by 20 U.S. companies, and about 34,000 "electric carriages" were on the road.[89]

Before World War I, over one third of motor vehicles on the road in America were electric, many powered by Thomas Edison's nickel-iron battery. In 1919, inventor Harry E. Dey introduced a vehicle with a unique integrated motor differential axle that allowed the motor to act as a generator and return power to the batteries while traveling downhill.[90] Detroit Electric Car Company was the last U.S. manufacturer of EVs.[91] A maker of custom-made EVs, the company went out of business in 1940 when its president died, taking the last vestige of the industry with it. In all, forty-six companies manufactured EVs between the late 1890s and Detroit Electric's demise.

What sold EVs was their range. Twenty-five to 40 miles was farther than most horse-drawn vehicles could go. At least two models also set speed records, traveling 66 mph over a one-kilometer course in 1899. But gas-powered vehicles were not to be left behind for long. Ironically, the development of the electric starter by Charles Kettering helped hasten the disappearance of electric vehicles.[92] This new device, which eliminated the need to hand-crank the engine in gasoline-powered vehicles, came along just as vehicles equipped with internal combustion engines were developing a greater range and as gas stations began to crop up.

Yet, though EVs largely disappeared from the American landscape, thousands—primarily delivery vehicles—remained in service in Europe,[93] and a small EV industry survived in other countries. In 1977, Japan had 13,000 and England some 30,000 electric vehicles in use.[94] In the 1960s, the Detroit automakers sponsored small R&D programs for EVs, and in the 1966 auto shows, GM unveiled the Electrovair, basically a Corvair conversion powered by silver-zinc batteries. Other American companies introduced prototype EVs, but high component costs and limited range and performance killed any commercial interest.

False starts did not snuff out all interest in EVs. In 1982, the city of Denver put six 40-foot battery-powered shuttle buses into service. Jointly developed by MCR of Goleta, California and Walter Vetter of West Germany, these buses were on the road just 14 months after contracts were signed,[95] and they have carried more than 12,000 people every day. Powered by four 2,500-pound Exide batteries each and reaching top speeds of just 20 mph, these buses are suitable only for mall-type or airport-shuttle service.

Electric buses are being tried elsewhere. In Chattanooga, Tennessee, seven electric buses were in service by the end of 1993 with an equal number to be added in 1994.[96] These buses are recharged overnight and have a top speed of 38 mph.

Worldwide, EV research and development activities have picked up recently too. The chief impetuses are the California Air Resources Board's low-emission-vehicle (LEV) regulations, the near-universal desire to reduce air pollution from motor vehicles, and the long-term need to curb carbon-dioxide emissions.

Recent U.S. Developments

In 1988, General Motors began work with inventor and engineer Paul MacCready of AeroVironment. Inc., on a sleek, powerful two-seater electric sports car, the Impact.[97] Unveiled at the Los Angeles auto show in January 1990, the car can go from 0 to 60 mph in 8 seconds, reach a top speed (electronically limited) of 75 mph, and—with a lead-acid battery—has a range of about 75 miles.

In April 1990, GM Chairman Roger Smith announced plans to produce and sell an EV for personal use. Eleven months later, the company announced that the Impact would be built in Lansing, Michigan, and introduced commercially in the mid-90s. In the words of Kenneth Baker, head of GM's EV program, "If you've been waiting for us, the waiting is over. We're committed to deliver a product by the mid '90s."[98] In December 1992, however, GM postponed mass-production of the Impact, scaling back manufacture to only 50 test vehicles. Thirty Impacts will be used in a two-year nationwide driving experiment in which 1,000 consumers will test-drive the vehicles for a few weeks. The target for mass production is now the late 1990s, still in time to comply with California's ZEV mandate.[99] Reportedly, the delay reflects the uncertain marketability of a two-seater sports car (which may be replaced by a more utilitarian, family-size vehicle[100]) and GM's continuing financial problems. Meanwhile, GM, Ford, and Chrysler are exploring joining forces through the U.S. Council for Automotive Research

(USCAR) to design, develop, test, and possibly manufacture EV components.

Ford's interest in electric vehicles dates back several decades.[101] From 1982 to 1985, it developed an electric version of its Escort, the ETX-I. In 1990, the company produced an electric version of its Aerostar van (ETX-II), equipping it with sodium-sulfur batteries that it had developed in the mid-1960s. The ETX-II has a range of 100 miles, a top speed of 65 mph, and a payload capacity of 1,000 pounds.

Also in 1990, Ford began work on its third generation of EVs. The Ecostar vans, conversions of Ford's European light-duty Escort van, have 56-kilowatt (kw) electric motors, advanced sodium-sulfur batteries, and AC powertrains. The vans have a payload of 900 to 1,000 pounds, a top speed of about 70 mph, a range of 100 miles (measured on the Federal Urban Driving Schedule, FUDS for short), and a 0-to-50 mph acceleration of 12 seconds. The vehicles sport ultra-efficient thermal glass and small fans powered by a strip of solar cells mounted along the windshield's upper edge to help ventilate the vehicles when they are parked in the sun. In November 1993, Ford begin leasing some 81 EV Ecostars for fleet testing over a thirty-month period, reportedly for $100,000 each.[102] Test data will be used to evaluate vehicle performance, the effects of climate variations, and infrastructure needs.[103]

Ford is developing other EVs too. At the 1992 Detroit Auto Show, an electric passenger vehicle named the Connector made its debut. Equipped with the same drive train and battery technology as the Ecostar, this vehicle is for urban driving. The Connector has one door on the driver's side, two doors on the passenger side, and fold-down rear seats to enhance cargo capacity.

In early 1993, Chrysler produced 50 electric test vehicles (Dodge Caravan Electrics) based on its popular minivan.[104] Powered by nickel-iron batteries, the minivan has an urban driving range of about 80 to 120 miles, a top speed of 65 mph, and accelerates from 0 to 30 mph in 8.25 seconds.[105] These prototype vehicles sell for $100,000 each (down $20,000 from 1993).[106] Their battery packs, priced at about $40,000, should last about 100,000 miles. Chrysler's next prototype EV, the TEVan II, will run on SAFT nickel-cadmium batteries, which have higher energy and power densities. In April 1992, Chrysler and Westinghouse announced a multi-million dollar joint venture to develop advanced EV propulsion systems.[107] With Norvik Technologies, Chrysler has also developed a quick-charging system that can recharge any battery (up to 95 percent) within 25 minutes without degrading it.

Detroit's Big Three aren't the only U.S. companies developing EV technology. AC Propulsion, Inc., a small California company started by two engineers who helped develop GM's Impact, converted a Honda CRX that achieved a range of 131 miles at a constant speed of 55 mph using lead-acid batteries in a test conducted by the California Air Resources Board (CARB) in March 1992.[108]

Most other small U.S. companies working on EVs[109] are primarily converting commercially available internal-combustion engine vehicles to EVs, though a few firms are manufacturing new EVs.[a] The Solectria Corporation of Wilmington, Massachusetts sells both EV components and converted conventional vehicles, mostly Geo Metros. Renamed the "Force," Solectria's electric vehicle is powered by a brushless DC motor and lead-acid or nickel-cadmium batteries. (An optional roof-mounted solar panel helps extend vehicle range and battery life.) U.S. Electricar, a publicly-owned conversion company in Sebastopol, California, has sold over 200 EVs to date and sells conversion kits. In April 1993, the company opened a new EV manufacturing plant in Los Angeles that will initially build about 50 electric cars a month and eventually that many per week.[110] Under the company's new agreements, Florida-based Consulier Automotive will manufacture a light-weight sports car using the Consulier GTP body. U.S. Electricar will design and install the EV system and the car will cost about $75,000.[111]

Other small companies either converting conventional vehicles or manufacturing EVs from scratch include California Electric Cars (Seaside, CA), Sebring Auto-Cycle (Sebring, FL), Electric Vehicles Corporation (Van Nuys, CA), Solar Car Corporation (Melbourne, FL), B.A.T. Technology (West Valley, UT), Triple "O" Seven Corp. (Everson, WA), Cushman, Inc., (Lincoln, NE), and Renaissance Cars, Inc. (Palm Beach, FL), which plans to begin manufacturing both a car

---

[a] The newsletter *Electric Vehicle Progress* (215 Park Avenue, South, Suite 1301, New York City) publishes a directory that lists all the companies producing EVs in the United States.

Box 5. Organizations Promoting EVs in the United States

The Washington D.C.-based Electric Transportation Coalition (ETC) is a non-profit coalition of electric utilities, automakers, various industries, unions, municipal and state agencies, and universities that promotes the use of electricity in transportation.[1] The Electric Vehicle Association of the Americas (EVAA) was founded in 1990 with a mission to promote EVs, to provide information, and to advance the electric and hybrid vehicles.[2]

---

1. Electric Transportation Coalition Organization Premises. Washington, D.C., n.d.
2. Electric Vehicle Association of the Americas, Mission Statement, n.d.

(the Tropica, a $10,000 two-seater capable of reaching 65 mph and ranging 60 to 80 miles per charge) and a light truck (at about $12,000).[112] Renaissance plans to build about 120 vehicles per month.

Federal Support

The Department of Energy is the main source of federal funds for EV research and development. DOE's Electric and Hybrid Vehicle Program works with industry to support basic and applied research on EV technology. DOE also funds an extensive program that gives universities, utility companies, national labs, and other federal agencies a chance to purchase various types of EVs for fleet testing. Within the Department of Defense, the Advanced Research Projects Agency is supporting a two-year cost-shared program ($25 million the first year) to find out how useful and efficient electric and hybrid vehicles are for military use: six consortia will develop electric trucks and buses. Battery and flywheel research is also being supported.

EV Programs in Other Countries

Battery-powered EVs are being developed overseas as well. In Japan in the late 1970s, the Ministry of International Trade and Industry (MITI) established the Electric Vehicle Council, the Japan Electric Vehicle Association (JEVA), and the Electric Vehicle Engineering Research Association (EVERA) to work with private industry to promote EV research, development, and commercialization.[113] The Council, which announced a market expansion program in October 1991, hopes to introduce 200,000 electric vehicles cumulatively by the year 2000 and 100,000 vehicles every year after, initially by targeting national and municipal governments, and from 1994 through 1997 by developing a nationwide EV infrastructure and offering tax breaks and other incentives to private users of EVs. From 1998 to 2000, retail prices will be lowered to capture the consumer market: the goal is to get EV costs down to within 20 percent of those of comparable conventional vehicles. In this stepwise plan, the focus after the year 2000 will be on cost reductions, technical advances, and infrastructure refinements. JEVA will disseminate information, participate in auto shows, study EV use in urban areas, study battery swapping, develop uniform standards for EVs, and take on other activities relating to EV leasing, public education, and data collection.

In Europe, EVs are also on the road to commercial use. The European Electric Road Vehicle Association (AVERE) promotes the widespread use of electric and hybrid vehicles by supporting research and analysis of advanced drive-train systems, energy storage and conversion devices (batteries, fuel cells, flywheels), chargers, safety, and environmental and regulatory issues.[114] CITELEC (a cooperative organization of European cities interested in electric vehicles) looks at the challenges of introducing EVs in urban areas, develops EV demonstration programs, evaluates new vehicles, and promotes development projects. CITELEC's demonstration programs will determine whether EVs can pass the acid test of urban traffic.[115]

In Germany, the Federal Ministry for Research and Technology (BMFT) has been testing the newest EVs on Rügen Island in the Baltic Sea since October 1992. The 60 test sedans, buses, and vans are equipped with sodium sulfur, sodium nickel chloride, nickel cadmium, or lead gel batteries. Battery recharging takes place mostly at night in residential garages or fleet parking places.[116] Meanwhile, Volkswagen recently announced its second-generation new Golf CityStromer, an electric van with power-assisted steering, an auxiliary heater, and a maximum payload of 630 kg (1,390 pounds). Now being tested, this van has a range of 120 km (74 miles) and a top speed of 105 km/h (65 mph).[117]

In France, Citröen is developing a modular vehicle, the CITELA (CITy ELectric Automobile), that uses nickel-cadmium batteries to achieve a top speed of 110 km/hr (68 mph), an acceleration of 0 to 50 km/hr (31 mph) in 8.5 seconds, a highway range of 210 km (130 miles), and an urban range of 110 km (68 miles). And a fleet of 80 Peugeot two-ton vans now serves 25 French cities. In the city of La Rochelle, PSA Peugeot Citröen and Electricité de France are working with the municipal government to introduce EVs. They have set up an Evaluation and Applied EV Research Center (CERAVE) to evaluate EVs, components, and batteries and serve as the technical advisor to the city.[118] PSA Peugeot Citröen is leasing 50 Peugeot 106 and Citröen AX electric vehicles for a demonstration program managed by the city council and CERAVE,[119] and the company has more than 500 orders for these two models, scheduled for delivery by 1995. The Citela, powered by nickel-cadmium batteries, will come out in the late 1990s.

Renault introduced electric vans commercially in 1993. Its Master is powered by lead-acid batteries with a range of 80 km (50 miles) or by nickel-cadmium batteries with a range of 120 km (75 miles). The range of the Express/Rapid van is 45 km (28 miles) with lead acid batteries and 110 km (68 miles) with nickel-cadmium batteries. Currently, 50 of these vans have logged over 310,000 miles in field tests. A dedicated EV, slated for production in 1995, is in development along with a prototype hybrid electric vehicle utilizing a gas turbine engine.[120] Renault's newest vehicle is the Zoom, a futuristic-looking EV with an urban driving range of 150 km (93 miles) and a chassis comprised of two moving parts.[121]

To reduce air pollution, the city of Paris has adopted an ambitious program to introduce EVs. The municipal government plans to have 200 EVs in its fleet by late 1995. Over 100 charging posts will be installed by the end of 1994 and regulations authorizing cheaper parking for EVs have been adopted.

Between 1992 and 1994, the French government increased its EV R&D program from $40 million to $100 million. These funds will support research on batteries and fuel cells, as well as EV demonstrations. Because most of France's electricity comes from nuclear power, EV use would significantly reduce air pollution.[122]

Status of Battery Development

Chemical or electro-mechanical batteries are likely to power electric vehicles unless—or until—hydrogen-powered fuel cells become technologically feasible and economically attractive. More than any other factor, the absence of low-cost, high energy-density, lightweight, long-lasting batteries inhibits the commercialization of electric vehicles. Work on regenerative braking, electronic controls, heaters, and air conditioners is also needed, but these challenges are relatively straightforward by comparison. In electric vehicles, batteries provide not only the basic energy to power the car or truck, but also electricity for the air conditioning, heating, headlights, power steering, and audio systems, which are major energy consumers. According to Roberta Nichols of the Ford Motor Company, an EV that takes an average 8 kw of power to complete the federal urban driving cycle could require another 5 kw to run the heater during winter or 3.5 kw to keep the air conditioner going.[123] In either case, meeting these power demands is at the expense of the vehicle's range—one reason that the Advanced Research Projects Agency is supporting the development of more efficient heating and air-conditioning systems.

To give EVs anything like the range, speed, and acceleration of today's oil-powered vehicles, EV batteries will need higher energy and power densities, higher charging and discharging efficiencies, longer lifetimes, and lower costs. These batteries will also need to be readily recyclable and free of major environmental or public health risks.

Current off-the-shelf lead-acid batteries have an energy density of about 40 watt-hours per kilogram. For perspective, the energy density of gasoline is about 300 times as great. But there is more to the story than simple energy density. Electric motors and other EV components are vastly more efficient than those in conventional vehicles. Consumers really don't care about energy density. What they want is range, and prototype EVs have achieved a range of roughly 100 miles—between a third and a fourth those of oil-powered cars and trucks.

For the past century, almost all EVs developed for commercial use have used lead-acid batteries—basically, the same as ordinary car batteries. For decades, these have performed well enough for short hops, and there is much to recommend them: low-cost and abundant materials, years of technological development and manufacturing experience, safety, a well-developed servicing and recycling infrastructure, and continued performance improvements.[124] But the shortcomings of this familiar technology[125] may outweigh its proven advantages. Although more advanced designs overcome some of these problems, lead-acid batteries are heavy, they don't last long, their energy density is low, they require regular maintenance (adding water), they generate hydrogen, and they pose safety risks from accidental acid spills.

U.S. Advanced Battery Consortium

Many analysts consider better EV batteries the "make or break" factor. To scale this technological barrier, researchers are following many development paths at once, working on advanced lead-acid, nickel-iron, nickel-cadmium, nickel-metal hydride, nickel-hydrogen, sodium-sulfur, sodium nickel chloride, and lithium batteries.[126] To accelerate the development of these batteries, Chrysler, Ford, and GM formed the U.S. Advanced Battery Consortium (USABC) in January 1991. The Electric Power Research Institute (EPRI) joined in July, and in October 1991 DOE signed a cooperative agreement with USABC to match industry funding for battery development, dollar for dollar. In all, some $260 million will be spent over four years.

This consortium's mid-term goal is to get a battery with the properties shown in Table 1 into production in 1994.[127] (The status of various candidate batteries is also shown in Table 1.) The mid-term goals are achieving a power-to-weight ratio of 150-200 watts per kilogram of battery weight, an energy-to-volume ratio of 135 watt-hours per liter of battery, and an energy-to-weight ratio of 80 watt-hours per kilogram of battery. (A power-to-volume ratio of at least 250 watts per liter of battery volume is also prescribed, but this requirement will automatically be met if the other three conditions are.) Other goals are a minimum five-year lifetime, the capacity to cycle 600 times (to an 80 percent depth of discharge), and a cost of less than $150 per rated kilowatt-hour of deliverable electricity. Current lead-acid batteries provide energy and power densities that are typically half of those sought. As Table 1 shows, US-ABC's "long-term" goals (target date 1995) are even more ambitious: the lifetime doubles again and the power and energy densities increase by 2.5 times.

USABC has signed several cost-sharing contracts to support advanced battery development. In May 1992, the Ovonic Battery Co. of Troy, Michigan was awarded $18.5 million to develop a mid-term nickel-metal-hydride battery. In the second round of awards, announced in October 1992, W.R. Grace and Johnson Controls received contracts totalling $24.5 million to develop lithium-polymer battery systems, and Delco Remy and Valence Technology were also awarded contracts for work on lithium batteries while Saft America, Inc., received $17.3 million to develop a long-term lithium (metal)-sulfide battery.[128] Several of DOE's national labs—including the National Renewable Energy Laboratory, Lawrence Berkeley Laboratory, Sandia National Laboratory, Argonne National Laboratory, and the Idaho National Engineering Laboratory—have also won USABC support for advanced battery development. In early 1994, USABC awarded a $33-million dollar contract to 3M, Hydro Quebec, and Argonne National Lab to develop advanced lithium-polymer batteries.

Which (if any) of the batteries listed in Table 1 will power future EVs is anyone's guess. Each type has its advocates. But even though the research engineers and the marketplace will do the final sorting out, it still helps to understand the pros and cons of each option.

Alternatives to the Battery: Ultracapacitors and Flywheels

The *average* power that must be supplied by an EV battery is relatively low (10-25 kw). (Exact requirements depend upon vehicle efficiency and driving conditions.) But *peak* power requirements—

43

Table 1. USABC Technology Goals and Status of Current Batteries

	Mid-Term	Long-Term	Present Status
Specific Power (W/kg)	150	400	
Lead-Acid			67–138
Nickel-Iron			70–132
Nickel-Cadmium			100–200
Nickel-Metal Hydride			200
Sodium Sulfur			90–130
Sodium Nickel Chloride			150
Lithium Polymer			100
Energy Density (Wh/L)	135	300	
Lead-Acid			50–82
Nickel-Iron			60–115
Nickel-Cadmium			60–115
Nickel-Metal Hydride			152–215
Sodium Sulfur			76-120
Sodium Nickel Chloride			160
Lithium Polymer			100–120
Specific Energy (Wh/kg)	80	200	
Lead-Acid			18–56
Nickel-Iron			39–70
Nickel-Cadmium			33–70
Nickel-Metal Hydride			54–80
Sodium Sulfur			80–140
Sodium Nickel Chloride			100
Lithium Polymer			150

	Mid-Term	Long-Term	Present Status
Life (years)	5	10	
Lead-Acid			2–3
Nickel-Iron			
Nickel-Cadmium			
Nickel-Metal Hydride			10
Sodium Sulfur			
Sodium Nickel Chloride			5
Lithium Polymer			
Cycle Life (80% DOD)	600	1000	
Lead-Acid			450–1000
Nickel-Iron			440–2000
Nickel-Cadmium			1500–2000
Nickel-Metal Hydride			1000
Sodium Sulfur			250–600
Sodium Nickel Chloride			600
Lithium Polymer			300
Ultimate Cost ($/kWh)	<$150	<$100	
Lead-Acid			70–100
Nickel-Iron			160–300
Nickel-Cadmium			300
Nickel-Metal Hydride			200
Sodium Sulfur			100+
Sodium Nickel Chloride			>350
Lithium Polymer			50-500

Box 6. Comparison of Promising Electric Batteries

Advanced Lead-Acid Batteries

Despite their many drawbacks, lead-acid batteries are still in the race for mid-term EV applications. Indeed, one under development by Horizon Battery Technologies, Inc., of Austin, Texas with support from the Electric Power Research Institute might reach USABC's mid-term goals,[1] and production of some 20,000 is projected for 1994. Certainly, the performance profile of the Horizon battery looks good. According to the manufacturer, this battery can be recharged 50 percent within 8 minutes, it can be cycled 900 times, it has an energy density of about 45 Wh/kg, it can be readily recycled,[2] and it is sealed and maintenance-free. It is projected to power a typical EV for 80 to 100 miles per charge and to last 80,000 miles. Chrysler plans to test the Horizon battery in its electric minivan.

To give superior lead-acid batteries (so-called Valve-Regulated Batteries, VRB) a push, the Advanced Lead-Acid Battery Consortium (ALABC) was formed with a four-year, $19.3-million research budget.[3] Developed more than twenty years ago, these second-generation lead-acid batteries require no maintenance, pose no hazard of acid spills, and have much higher energy and power densities than ordinary lead-acid batteries.

Nickel-Cadmium Batteries (Ni-Cd)

Ni-Cd batteries are already in use in some Japanese and European EVs. Originally developed in small sizes for various consumer applications,[4] Ni-Cd batteries are more expensive than lead-acid batteries (because nickel is costly). But they offer higher energy density, and they can be recharged at least a thousand times. Although the battery can be "quick-charged," recharging efficiency is poor at high temperatures (a major technical drawback), and elaborate thermal defenses are needed to avoid overheating.[5] Also, cadmium is highly toxic, so its use—from manufacture to recycling—would have to be managed carefully.

Nickel-Iron Batteries (Ni-Fe)

Some nickel-iron batteries have a high energy density and are long lasting.[6] And research now underway could make these batteries more efficient, reduce hydrogen production (a potential safety problem), and eliminate the need to add water periodically. The battery appears to be capable of over 1,000 deep-discharge cycles before performance degradation suffers.[7]

Sodium-Sulfur Batteries (Na-S)

Na-S batteries are emerging as a promising mid-term battery technology because of their high power- and energy-densities, low maintenance needs, low self-discharge, long service-life, excellent electrical characteristics, and low materials costs. Currently, sodium-sulfur research is being supported by Eagle-Picher Industries, Inc., Chloride Silent Power, Ltd. (U.K.), Asea Brown Boveri (Sweden, Germany, Switzerland) and its Canadian subsidiary, Powerplex, and RWE (Germany).

Na-S batteries must be pre-heated to high temperatures, 300–350°C, (570–660°F) and kept there during use. The batteries are housed in insulated double-walled vacuum containers, and if the electrodes solidify from non-use, built-in heaters can re-melt the sodium and sulfur. The main technical challenges still to be met are reducing premature cell failure,[8] extending battery life, reducing costs,[9] and ensuring safety under both routine operating conditions and during accidents. Since sodium and sulfur are relatively cheap, sodium-sulfur batteries could be economically competitive over the long term.

Sodium Nickel Chloride Batteries (NaNiCl$_2$)

The NaNiCl$_2$ battery is a high-temperature (300°C) battery that its manufacturer, AEG Anglo Batteries, claims is maintenance free, can operate even if individual cells fail, and is safe in accidents.[10] As Table 1 shows, the NaNiCl$_2$ battery meets USABC's midterm energy- and power-density goals. Existing batteries have cycled 600 times and AEG hopes to reach 1,000

(continues on next page)

Box 6. *(continued)*

cycles by 1998. A life of five years is expected. If allowed to cool down, the battery can be reheated (albeit in 48 hours) without damage so long as no power is drawn when the battery temperature is below about 270°C. Still, costs are a problem: the price is predicted to be two and a half times ($375/kWh) US-ABC's mid-term goal ($150/kWh). In Germany, BMW, Mercedes Benz, VW, and Opel are all testing EVs powered by sodium nickel chloride batteries.

Nickel-Metal-Hydride Batteries (NiMH)

NiMH batteries offer more than twice the energy density (Wh/kg) of lead-acid batteries and a three-to-one advantage in volumetric energy density (Wh/L). According to Ovonic Battery Company, current batteries have achieved an energy density of 80 Wh/kg and a peak power of 175 W/kg at 80-percent depth-of-discharge.[11] Battery life is expected to reach 2,000 to 3,000 cycles at an 80-percent depth-of-discharge.

A switch from lead-acid to advanced NiMH batteries would greatly boost EV performance. In GM's Impact EV, the substitution would increase the car's range to 300 miles, and the NiMH batteries would probably last as long as the car.[12] NiMH batteries can withstand overcharge and over-discharge abuse. They also exhibit a long cycle-life and high power density. They can be recharged rapidly and require no maintenance. The manufacturer claims the battery is environmentally friendly and 100-percent recyclable as well.[13] In May 1992, the USABC announced its first cost-shared contract award to Ovonic to scale up the company's NiMH technology to EV battery-pack size. Eleven months later, it placed a $1.4-million order for prototype NiMH batteries for testing in electric vehicles.[14]

Nickel-Hydrogen Batteries

Nickel-hydrogen batteries are used in communications satellites. They offer excellent energy density, they can tolerate considerable abuse, and they are highly reliable in EV applications.[15] Moreover, they can be overcharged and over-discharged without damage. The battery also has the built-in equivalent of a gasoline gauge—internal hydrogen pressure that can be "read." These batteries are fairly expensive, partly because they now require complex hand assembly. But they are becoming cost competitive, especially in applications requiring more than 10,000 cycles. Longevity is another plus: the batteries could be guaranteed for the life of the vehicle.

Lithium-Polymer Electrolyte Batteries

Lithium batteries are a more distant option for providing high energy- and power-densities. Over the years, research has focused on developing a safe, high-energy battery, and recently safety characteristics have improved.[16] A major remaining challenge is scaling up small batteries to vehicle-size units. Valence Technology Inc. and other firms are currently developing lithium batteries, which are expected to operate efficiently over a broad range of temperatures.[17] The USABC and the Commission of the European Communities are both supporting research on these battery systems.

Other Battery Technologies

Research continues on other battery and electrical storage technologies too. Zinc-air batteries look especially attractive. An Israeli firm, Electric Fuel, Limited, has developed a very powerful zinc-air battery that can be "recharged" in three minutes by replacing the electrodes, which are later recycled for further use.[18] The battery has an energy density of 207 Wh/kg, about ten times that of lead batteries. The German postal service has been testing these batteries with promising results: soon it will try them in 40 vans, and over time it plans to convert 80 percent of its fleet to EVs that can use them.

Three promising battery systems for EVs currently under development in the United States and abroad are lithium aluminum-iron sulfide, iron-air, and aluminum-air.

(continues on next page)

Box 6. *(continued)*

1. Electric Power Research Institute. "Advanced Electric Vehicle Lead-Acid Battery Project," 1993.

2. Electrosource, Inc. "Horizon, Advanced Lead-Acid Battery Technology, Technical Summary," 1993.

3. Nelson, R.F. and D. Rand. "Putting Your Best Foot Forward—A Blueprint for a Lead-Acid Battery Technology and Infrastructure for Electric Vehicles." EVS-11, Florence, Italy, 1992.

4. Personal Communication with D. McArthur, December 15, 1992.

5. Bourg, A. "Batteries for Electric Vehicles—General Perspectives." EVS-11, 1992.

6. Electric Power Research Institute. "Battery Development for Electric Vehicles," 1990.

7. Coates D. and L. Miller. "Advanced Batteries for Electric Vehicle Applications." EVS-11, 1992.

8. Bourge, A. "Batteries for Electric Vehicles—General Perspectives." EVS 11, 1992.

9. Sandia National Laboratory. "Power Sources," 1991.

10. Hammerling, H. et al. "ZEBRA Batteries to Power Tomorrow's Electric Vehicles" presented at Hawaii EV '93, December 9–12, 1993, Honolulu.

11. Ovshinsky, S.R., et.al. "A Nickel Metal Hydride Battery for Electric Vehicles." *Science*, Vol. 260, pp. 176–81, EVS-11, April 9, 1993.

12. Ovshinsky, S.R., et al. "Performance Advances in Ovonic Nickel-Metal Hydride Batteries for Electric Vehicles." EVS-11, Sept. 1992.

13. Ovonic Battery Company, Troy, Michigan. "Questions and Answers," n.d.

14. USABC. "Battery Consortium Purchases Prototype Batteries." Press Release, April 21, 1993.

15. Coates, D. and L. Miller. "Advanced Batteries for Electric Vehicles," EVS-11, Sept. 1992.

16. Personal Communication with D. McArthur. December 15, 1992.

17. Montgomery Securities. "Prospectus," Valence Technology, Inc. Nov. 2, 1992.

18. Lossau, N. "Germany's Post Vans Go Electric." *New Scientist*. Jan. 22, 1994.

relatively short bursts of energy needed to climb hills or to accelerate rapidly—can be more than ten times greater.[129] EV batteries must thus be designed to meet both the energy (kw-hrs) and peak-power (kw) demands if drivers are to get the range and acceleration they expect. But these two needs can be decoupled—and the power requirements for EV batteries relaxed—if the battery load is leveled using a secondary storage device (such as an ultracapacitor or flywheel) to help meet peak power needs.[130] Such a device would be charged with electricity from the EV's primary battery during normal EV operation. During rapid acceleration, this "banked" power would be withdrawn.

Ultracapacitors

A capacitor is an electrical component (found in almost all radios, TVs, power supplies, and other appliances) that can store electrical energy. An ultracapacitor is simply a capacitor that can store large amounts of energy. Because these devices do not depend on chemical reactions, capacitors can be charged and discharged far more rapidly than batteries.

The U.S. Department of Energy supports research and testing of ultracapacitors for EVs and other applications through its Office of Energy Efficiency and Renewable Energy. The main goals are improving ultracapacitor energy densities and lengthening their lifetimes. Existing ultracapacitors almost meet DOE's short-term goals, and the long-term goals may be achieved within five years.[131] The development of powerful ultracapacitors would greatly improve the performance and range of EVs. (An ultracapacitor meeting the long-term goal could take a car from 0 to 55 mph in 8 seconds.) If truly high-performance ultracapacitors were developed, they could even replace EV batteries altogether, making the long charging times that are unavoidable with traditional batteries a thing of the past.

Flywheels

Flywheels could also supply electric power for EVs. Their proponents claim that these devices have the potential to outperform chemical storage batteries in every important way.[132] The rationale for using flywheels is exactly the same as for ultracapacitors: initially, they could level the load placed on the vehicle's battery, thereby relaxing the battery's power requirements. Used in this way, flywheels could extend the range of a battery-powered EV by 30 percent in urban driving. Super powerful flywheels could eventually replace the chemical battery —ending any potential threat of chemical releases—and be recharged directly from the power grid.

The principle of the flywheel is quite simple: a rotating object (such as a potter's wheel) possesses kinetic energy that can be converted to electrical energy. Magnets placed on the rotating wheel generate power as their magnetic fields cross wires surrounding the wheel, and this process is reversible: by applying power to the surrounding wires, the flywheel can be made to rotate faster and faster, storing more and more mechanical energy.

Electro-mechanical (EMB) batteries, as flywheels are called, are expected to reach specific energy densities as high as 150 Wh/kg, close to USABC's long-term goal for chemical batteries.[133] *(See Table 1.)* More impressive still are these devices' very high power densities (5,000 to 10,000 W/kg)—more than ten times the USABC's long-term goal of 400 W/kg. Pound for pound, flywheels pack more than ten times as much power as a V-8 engine and more than seventy times as much as a lead-acid battery. Clearly, power would be ample for accelerating EVs. EMBs could also be used in stationary applications to store electricity from renewable sources of power, such as wind turbines or photovoltaic cells.

To reduce internal power losses, the rotor of an EMB would spin on magnetic bearings in a vacuum chamber at about 200,000 RPM. Running with essentially no friction, it would take many weeks for flywheels to self discharge.[134] Other advantages: the devices should last the life of the vehicle,[135] they could be recharged in 5 to 10 minutes, they could be used with regenerative braking, and they are highly efficient in storing electric power.

High energy-densities are achieved by making the EMBs relatively small, about the size of a conventional storage battery, but with very high rotation speeds. Each flywheel can store about a kw-hr of electrical energy.[136] In an accident or failure, the graphite fiber-composite rotor would disintegrate into a mass of relatively harmless "cotton candy"—rather than shrapnel—says Richard Post, a flywheel developer at DOE's Lawrence Livermore Lab.[137]

Flywheels for use in EVs are being developed by several companies, including American Flywheel Systems (AFS), based in Washington, Unique Mobility of Colorado, and Flywheel Energy Systems of Ontario, Canada. AFS patented its flywheel design in 1992, and in March 1993 it asked Honeywell to build it a working flywheel within two years.[138] In May 1993, AFS received $2 million from California and federal agencies to help underwrite its flywheel development efforts.[139] In September 1993, the company demonstrated a working Honeywell-built flywheel; AFS hopes to have a prototype that automakers can test in 1994. In late 1993, AFS joined with TDM, International, a Michigan-based automotive engineering firm, to build an electric vehicle powered by flywheels. Meanwhile, Unique Mobility is conducting flywheel research on vehicle applications with several companies, including United Technologies Corporation and Flywheel Energy Systems.

Hybrid Vehicles

To increase range, hybrid electric vehicles that supplement the electricity from batteries using other energy sources, such as on-board gasoline-powered engines, are being developed. (Sometimes, the term hybrid covers any vehicle that employs more than one energy source—such as fuel cells, ultracapacitors, and flywheels—to supplement batteries, but as used here the term refers only to vehicles with carbon-fuel-burning engines on board.)

Hybrids are designed to operate as EVs in urban areas where air pollution is a problem. Operating on batteries alone, they typically have a range of 50 to 100 miles. (For perspective here, the total distance traveled by all the cars in an average U.S. household is only 41 miles per day.[140]) These vehicles could well operate solely as EVs for more than 90 percent of the time, reserving their engines for longer trips.

Hybrids have several advantages over either gasoline-powered vehicles or battery-powered EVs. Since hybrid engines are designed for average loads, not peak loads, they can be relatively small and run at a constant speed while charging the EV batteries. Hybrids can be more than twice as efficient and much less polluting than comparable internal combustion engine vehicles.[141] Typically equipped with batteries and regenerative brakes, hybrids can capture much of the energy normally lost in braking, further increasing overall fuel efficiency. An on-board engine makes the vehicle's range far greater than that of a battery-powered EV, increasing consumer acceptance. Still, hybrids are not ZEVs. Unless the on-board energy source is hydrogen, they still emit air pollutants.

Moreover, since the emissions performance of combustion engines tends to deteriorate over time, air pollution emissions will probably increase as the vehicles age. Hybrids are also more complicated and—with two power systems on board—more expensive to build. Another drawback: although the California Air Resources Board allows fuel-burning heaters in ZEVs, hybrids do not qualify. As a result, hybrid vehicles are sometimes characterized as transitional vehicles—useful mainly until more powerful batteries or other storage devices are developed.

Hybrids are being developed by automakers both here and overseas. In separate awards, DOE has chosen GM and Ford to develop prototype hybrid vehicles. In September 1993, DOE awarded GM a (50–50) cost-shared $138-million contract; in December, it gave a $122-million contract to a group led by Ford. DOE hopes to spur the development of vehicles that have dramatically improved fuel efficiency and comply with pollution-emission standards without costing more or performing less well than conventional vehicles. Production of these vehicles would begin sometime after 2001.

To spur the introduction of EVs, the Los Angeles City Council in 1988 approved a motion establishing the Los Angeles Electric Vehicle Initiative. *(See Box 7.)* Through the Los Angeles Department of Water and Power with help from Southern California Edison, the city hoped to subsidize the introduction of 10,000 hybrids by 1995. One prototype—a four-passenger, 2-door hatchback—was built and tested. It has sealed lead-acid batteries and a 45-hp engine burning reformulated gasoline to charge the batteries at high speeds.[142] On batteries, the range is about 60 miles; with the gasoline engine, about 150 miles. But the Swedish manufacturer, Clean Air Transport couldn't raise the capital needed for tooling and manufacturing, and in January 1994 filed for bankruptcy. Meanwhile, the original Los Angeles EV initiative has evolved into a comprehensive infrastructure-development program aimed at getting electric vehicles into use.

In Colorado, Unique Mobility has built a prototype hybrid EV based on Chrysler's minivan.[143] The alternator that charges the battery is powered by a 2-cylinder 12-horsepower Honda engine that will run on propane, natural gas, or methanol.[144] Unique Mobility and Alupower Canada Ltd. are jointly developing an hybrid—an-

Box 7. L.A. Plugs into Electric Vehicles

In July 1991, Los Angeles adopted a 10-point plan to encourage the use of electric vehicles:

1. Providing charging facilities and preferred parking for employees who drive EVs.
2. Developing individual metering for EV charging.
3. Adopting building codes so that future homes have adequate EV recharging facilities.
4. Asking employers with more than 100 parking spaces to provide preferred parking or charging power for EVs.
5. Asking other counties and utilities to adopt similar programs.
6. Asking airport officials to use EVs (as, for instance, shuttle vans) and to set aside EV parking spaces.
7. Informing employers of EV credits for car-pool programs.
8. Supporting state legislation for preferred on-street parking for EVs.
9. Requiring all park-and-ride lots to set aside a certain number of spaces for EV users.
10. Asking public transportation agencies to install charging stations at various stops.

For further information contact the Los Angeles Department of Water and Power at 1-800-552-2334 or 213-367-0339.

other Chrysler minivan conversion—in which the lead-acid batteries would be charged during driving by an aluminum-air power cell.[145] In this cell, electricity is generated through chemical reactions between aluminum, water, and oxygen (from the air) to form a dry powder. Periodically, the aluminum compound is removed and recycled back into pure aluminum for reuse in another car. The vehicle is expected to have a range of about 190 miles and a top speed of 60 mph.

Worldwide, engineers are hard at work on hybrids. In Germany, Audi and Volkswagen both have active programs. Audi's prototype uses a conventional gasoline engine to drive the front wheels while the rear wheels are powered by an electric motor operating from nickel-cadmium batteries.[146] The car is mainly for urban short trips since the top speed is only 30 mph and the range a modest 20 miles. Volkswagen's new prototype hybrids are based on its Golf automobile using a diesel engine.[147] Magnet-Motor, GmbH, also of Germany, has developed a hybrid electric bus featuring a diesel engine (about one third the size of a normal bus engine) that under cruise conditions operates an electric generator to power the bus. A flywheel provides the extra boost needed to accelerate or climb hills. Experimental buses using this technology are on the streets in Munich. Diesel-electric buses are also being tested in Milan, Italy. In Sweden, Volvo unveiled a gas-turbine hybrid with a range of 50 miles while operating on batteries.

EV Performance and Life-Cycle Cost Estimates

Achieving the USABC's goals would go a long way toward making EVs acceptable to the driving public. Higher battery energy-densities would extend the range of EVs, and higher power densities and improvements in electric motors would provide the acceleration needed to approach the performance of conventional gasoline-powered vehicles. Longer battery lifetimes (1,000 cycles at 80 percent depth-of-discharge) and lower costs (less than $100 per rated kilowatt-hour) would help put EVs on an economic par with conventional vehicles.

The economics of EVs using existing technologies don't look good at the moment, at least in the United States.[148] The high costs and relatively short lifetimes of present batteries, as well as the low price of gasoline, combine to make the costs of driving an EV considerably higher than those of conventional vehicles. Even achieving USABC's long-term goals would not guarantee economic parity if gasoline prices remain at near all-time lows. *(See Box 8 and Figure 10.)*

For sound reasons, the price of gasoline should be higher than its current $1.20 or so per gallon. For one, drivers of cars and trucks in the United States are heavily, if indirectly, subsidized: they do not pay, out of pocket, many of the external costs they impose on society including those of air pollution, climate risks, national security threats, and noise.[149] If these costs were reflected at the fuel pump, the price of motor vehicle fuels would rise by at least $0.55 per gallon, and the annual cost of operating a gasoline minivan *(see Box 8)* would increase by about $305. Of course, EVs also impose social costs, such as carbon-dioxide emissions from power-plants which contribute to global warming. But these costs are much less than those of gasoline cars. If the EVs were recharged with the present national mix of power plants, and a carbon tax of $60 per ton of carbon were imposed, these costs would total about $56 per year. If the social costs of both vehicles are taken into account, the annual life cycle costs of the two vehicles are just about equal.

Life-cycle costs between the vehicles could also be equalized if battery costs were to drop below the USABC goal of $100 per kw-hr, even if fuel prices remained where they are now. If the externalities of each vehicle are ignored and battery costs were brought down to $73 per rated kw-hr, the two vehicles would cost about the same amount to buy and run.

Figure 11 shows estimated annual fuel- and battery-costs for gasoline and electric vehicles under a variety of assumptions. In the **Base Case**, battery-development goals are met, electricity prices are $0.05 per kw-hr, and gasoline sells for $1.20 per gallon. In this scenario, the EV would cost about $243 more per year to own and operate than a similar gasoline vehicle.

Case A illustrates what would happen if a sizable carbon tax of $60 per ton of carbon were placed on all fossil fuels. The price of electricity (assuming the average national mix of fuels) would rise by about 20 percent (1.2 cents per kw-hr) and the price of gasoline would increase about 15 cents per gallon. The cost of operating both EVs and gasoline vehicles would increase as a result, but the EV annual cost would still be about $217 higher than that for the gasoline vehicle.

In **Case B**, the goals for reducing battery costs are not met and batteries cost $125 per kw-hr, compared to $100 in the base case. Fuel prices are the same as in the base case. Under these circumstances, the annual cost of the EV increases to $466 over the gasoline vehicle.

Box 8. Comparing the Costs of an EV and a Comparable Gasoline Vehicle

Toying with the idea of switching to an electric vehicle? Consider the following simple comparison between the cost of driving Chrysler's gasoline-powered minivan and that of its EV version, the Dodge Caravan Electric. Optimistically, assume for starters that USABC's long-term goals for battery cost and performance are met *(see Table 1)* and that initially the two vehicles (excluding the EV battery pack) cost the same—say, $20,000. If the EV is to have a minimally acceptable range of 125 miles per charge (the range of present Caravan EVs) and if the Caravan uses 0.44 kw-hrs per mile (measured at the wall outlet), electricity consumption is 55 kw-hrs (125 x 0.44) to drive 125 miles. If the battery is to be discharged by no more than 80 percent from its peak, then the battery's total capacity must be 55/.8 = 68.7 kw-hrs. To determine the battery's cost, take the USABC's long-term goal of $100 per kw-hr of capacity. The initial cost of the EV battery—and therefore the extra cost of the electric vehicle—would then be about $6,875.

If the battery meets USABC's goal of 1,000 cycles, equivalent to driving 125,000 miles, it should last the life of the EV. If the van lasts 10 years, financing the battery pack (over 10

Case C combines Cases A and B: a carbon tax of $60 per ton of carbon is enacted, and the battery goals are not met. Here too, the EV's annual cost is greater than that of the gasoline vehicle, this time by $440.

In **Case D**, the EV battery goals are met, but instead of a carbon tax a gasoline tax of $0.50 per gallon is levied (roughly, the current unpaid social costs of gasoline). In this case, the annual costs are about equal.

This simplified comparison shows the importance to EVs' economic viability of battery performance, cost, and lifetime; the availability of the federal tax credit to reduce the EV purchase years) at a 5-percent interest rate costs about $890 per year. The electricity cost for operating the EV can also be readily estimated. At 10,000 miles per year and 0.44 kw-hrs per mile, the electric van would consume 4,400 kw-hrs. At an assumed (off-peak) electric rate of $0.05 per kw-hr, the electricity bill would be $220 per year. Batteries and electricity for the EV would thus cost about $1,110 per year.

If gasoline continues to cost about $1.20 per gallon, the gasoline version of the van averages 18 mpg in the city,[a] and the van travels 10,000 miles per year (consuming 555 gallons per year), the annual gasoline bill would be $667. To this, add $200 for such additional maintenance as oil changes, tune ups, etc. that an EV doesn't need. In all, the total annual cost for the gasoline van (excluding the purchase cost, insurance, license fees, common maintenance costs, etc.) is $867. Under these assumptions, the EV would cost about $243 more per year to own and operate than the gasoline version. *(See Base Case in Figure 11.)* This gap would narrow if gas prices rose or if battery prices dropped below the $100 per kw-hr.

---

[a] This is a very optimistic value estimated by EPA. Consumers Union measures the minivan's fuel efficiency at 11 to 12 mpg in city driving. *Consumer Reports*, October 1992, February 1993.

price; electricity and gasoline prices; and the economic externalities associated with the two vehicles. It also highlights an important barrier to EV ownership: the higher purchase price. In the example considered above, the EV would cost about 35 percent more to purchase (almost $7,000)—a major hurdle to overcome. Experience with other high purchase-price, low operating-cost technologies—such as compact fluorescent light bulbs—suggests that consumer resistance to paying higher initial costs is high.

Independent economic analyses confirm that EVs cost more to buy and operate than their gasoline counterparts. One study concluded that the cost of operating an EV van in the United States is

Figure 11. Annual Costs of EVs and Gasoline Vehicles

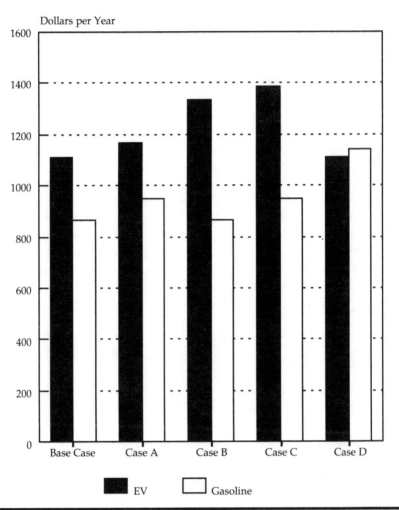

about 70 percent more per mile than that of a conventional vehicle,[150] partly because gasoline prices are so low in the United States. In another analysis, DeLuchi compared estimated costs of future mass-produced EVs powered by both batteries and hydrogen fuel-cells to the costs of advanced gasoline-powered vehicles.[151]

Comparing vehicles on a life-cycle cost-per-mile basis, and estimating the break-even price of gasoline that would yield equal life-cycle costs, he concluded (in his base case) that battery-powered EVs with an effective range of 60 miles would be cost-competitive with conventional vehicles at a gasoline price of $1.50 per gallon (including all fuel taxes.) If the EV had a range of 250 miles, the extra batteries would increase the EV life-cycle cost by about 7 percent. In this case, the breakeven price of gasoline would have to be $2.11 per gallon.

Estimates by experts aside, the public apparently expects EVs to actually cost *less* than their gasoline counterparts. Industry polls suggest that potential EV owners—recognizing the restricted performance of present EVs—will be willing to pay no more than 85 percent of the corresponding cost of gasoline vehicles.[152] Studies conducted by researchers at the University of California, Davis, however, are much more optimistic, concluding that modest incentives would readily lead to consumers' accepting the shorter range of EVs.

B. Hydrogen-Powered Electric Vehicles

Hydrogen is the lightest and most abundant element in the universe, constituting about 93 percent of all atoms.[153] The element is very reactive chemically and occurs as a free element only in trace amounts. On earth, it is found in water (H_2O), fossil fuels (basically, compounds of hydrogen and carbon), and all plants and animals.

Hydrogen gas (H_2) is not a primary fuel in the same sense as natural gas, oil, and coal are. No wells produce hydrogen gas from geologically identified deposits. Rather, hydrogen is an energy carrier. Like electricity, it is a secondary form of energy, produced using other, primary energy sources, such as natural gas or coal. Hydrogen can also be made from biomass or through electrolysis of water (H_2O) using electricity from renewable,[a] fossil, or nuclear power. Another advantage is that transporting hydrogen via

---

[a] Most renewable energy sources are intermittent: the winds do not always blow and the sun doesn't always shine. Using these technologies to generate hydrogen for later consumption will increase their availability and reliability.

pipelines over long distances costs less than transmitting high-voltage electricity.[154]

When hydrogen burns, it releases energy as heat and produces water ($2H_2 + O_2 \longrightarrow 2H_2O$). No carbon is involved, so using hydrogen as an energy source could eliminate carbon monoxide and ozone air pollution and reduce greenhouse warming. (Direct burning of hydrogen may still produce small amounts of nitrogen oxides, however.)

More than 8 million tons of hydrogen are consumed in the United States each year, primarily by the chemical and petroleum industries.[155] NASA also uses large quantities in the space-shuttle program. Most of this hydrogen is made from natural gas (mainly methane, CH_4) in a process called steam reforming. Smaller amounts are recovered from chlorine caustic cells or, if very pure hydrogen is required, generated by electrolysis. Since steam reforming depends on a depletable fossil fuel (natural gas) and releases the greenhouse gas carbon dioxide, the process is not sustainable over the long term. If the electric current in electrolysis were generated by a solar or nuclear source, carbon-dioxide emissions would not be a problem. If the electricity came from a renewable energy source, such as wind turbines or solar cells, the hydrogen would also be renewable and virtually limitless. But while electrolysis is a well-established technology, hydrogen made in this process is still quite expensive. Even if cheap hydropower is used, the cost is about twice that of hydrogen produced from natural gas.[156]

Hydrogen and Electricity: The Energy Carriers in a Sustainable Economy

Hydrogen and electricity can be considered opposite sides of the same coin. Electricity can be readily, if not cheaply, used to produce hydrogen via electrolysis.[a] Reversing the process, hydrogen can be consumed to produce pollution-free electricity via a fuel cell

---

[a] In modern electrolyzers, an electric current is passed through a solution of water and potassium hydroxide (KOH); hydrogen and oxygen are liberated at the two electrodes.

(which chemically combines hydrogen and oxygen to produce electricity, water, and waste heat). Though fuel cells were conceived in the 19th century, powerful versions were not developed until 40 years ago. Unlike internal combustion engines, these battery-like devices involve no high-temperature combustion and thus produce none of the nitrogen oxides needed to form smog.

The most efficient way to use hydrogen to power vehicles is in fuel cells. The wheels of EVs equipped with these cells would be powered by electric motors and the vehicles would emit no air pollution. As attractive long-term alternatives to oil- or battery-powered cars and trucks, hydrogen vehicles using fuel cells offer other potential advantages too: low vehicle noise, long range, and—at least for some hydrogen storage systems—refueling in minutes. Such vehicles could play a key role in the evolution of a "hydrogen economy," one in which mainly hydrogen is used to store and transmit energy.

The long-term choice between using electricity to power vehicles or using hydrogen fuel cells—or both in the form of a battery/fuel-cell vehicle—depends on many factors. The relative costs of fuel generation, storage, and transmission must be considered along with the weight and safety of the relevant storage and conversion devices. If technological breakthroughs dramatically improve electricity storage in batteries, flywheels, or ultracapacitors, EVs powered by directly-stored electricity derived from non-fossil sources may prove to be the best long-term option. But if major improvements were to occur in hydrogen storage or fuel-cells, hydrogen fuel-cell vehicles could become the technology of choice. In either case, the vehicles themselves would emit no pollution. As long as the underlying electric power needed for either vehicle is generated by non-fossil sources, prospects for minimizing air pollution and global warming and for enhancing energy security would improve.

Sources of Hydrogen

The approximate costs of producing hydrogen from natural gas, coal, electrolysis, and biomass are shown in Table 2.[157] The cheapest source is steam reforming of natural gas. The production

---

Box 9. A Brief History of Hydrogen

According to hydrogen-historian Peter Hoffmann, the idea of using hydrogen as a power source is anything but new.[1] In 1800, the electrolysis of water was first attempted by Nicholson and Carlisle, two British scientists, just after the electric cell was invented.[2] Jules Verne, the father of science fiction, prophetically heralded hydrogen in his 1874 novel *The Mysterious Island*,[3] foreseeing the use of "water as a fuel for steamers and engines" after it was "decomposed into its primitive elements...by electricity."[4] In 1923, a young Scottish geneticist, J.B.S. Haldane, advocated storing wind-generated hydrogen as a liquid since liquefied hydrogen "gives about three times as much heat per pound as petrol."[5] In the 1930s, Franz Lawaczeck, a German turbine designer, proposed transporting hydrogen via pipeline, like natural gas. At about the same time, Rudolph Erren converted over 1,000 internal combustion engine vehicles to hydrogen and hydrogen/gasoline operation in England and Germany.

But then R&D activity on hydrogen all but ceased for 30 years. Francis Bacon revived interest in hydrogen in the 1950s with his work in fuel-cell technology.[6] In the late 1960s and early 1970s, Japan, West Germany, and the United States again began to fund hydrogen research. In 1966, sixteen-year old Roger Billings built the first hydrogen-powered vehicle in the United States.

U.S. automakers have invested relatively little in hydrogen fuel research, mainly because vehicles powered by batteries are easier to manufacture than hydrogen-fueled ones. Still, some small companies and universities are pressing forward on the hydrogen front. Since 1982, a fuel-cell/battery-operated hybrid bus has been under development at Georgetown University, and recently the Department of Transportation, the Federal Transit Administration, California's South Coast Air Quality Management District (SCAQMD), and DOE have chipped in financial support for the project. The phosphoric-acid fuel-cell powered buses are expected to have 50 percent higher fuel economy and 99 percent lower emissions and to be much quieter than diesel-powered buses.[7] The first of three buses, scheduled for testing in California, Washington, D.C., and Chicago, were delivered in February 1994.

In January 1993, Canada's Ballard Power Systems began testing a 20-passenger transit bus that runs on hydrogen and a 120-kilowatt proton-exchange-membrane (PEM) fuel cell and enjoys a range of about 94 miles. In West Palm Beach, Florida, a small company, Energy Partners, Inc., is researching fuel cells for use in motor vehicles with support from DOE and SCAQMD to develop a proof-of-concept lightweight car powered by a hydrogen fuel-cell. A prototype, the Green Car, was rolled out in October 1993.[8] Powered by a PEM fuel cell, the car can reach 60 mph and has a range of 60 miles in city driving.

In Europe, Daimler Benz has built hydrogen buses with metal-hydride storage systems. BMW is investigating liquid hydrogen using modified conventional vehicles, while Daimler Benz is experimenting with hydride storage systems. In the late 1970s, the German Aerospace Research and Testing Institute (DLR) began experimenting with liquid-hydrogen storage systems. During the mid-1980s, a multi-year demonstration and testing program involving gasoline/hydrogen and dedicated hydrogen vehicles took place in Berlin.[9]

In Japan, the Musashi Institute of Technology began conducting research involving liquid hydrogen in 1970. Since then, it has developed both a two-stroke engine and "glow-plug assisted" diesel engines[10] and has continued developing demonstration vehicles operating on liquid hydrogen.[11] Mazda, exploring hydrogen vehicles powered by both internal combustion engines and fuel cells,[12] has developed a concept car equipped with a PEM fuel cell and a metal-hydride storage tank.

Soviet scientists also conducted research on hydrogen vehicles, including automobiles and aircraft that operate on liquid

(continues on next page)

Box 9. *(continued)*

hydrogen. R&D efforts continue in the former Soviet republics despite cut-backs.[13] India, Poland, South Africa, Sweden, Italy, Australia, and Canada also have hydrogen research programs.[14]

1. Hoffmann, P. *The Forever Fuel: The Story of Hydrogen*, Westview Press, Boulder, CO., 1981.
2. Hoffmann, P. *The Forever Fuel: The Story of Hydrogen*. Westview Press, Boulder, CO., 1981.
3. Hoffmann, P. "Fueling the Future with Hydrogen." *The Washington Post*, Sept. 6, 1987.
4. Verne, J. *The Invisible Island*.
5. Hoffmann, P. "Fueling the Future with Hydrogen," *The Washington Post*, Sept. 6, 1987.
6. U.S. Department of Energy, "Fundamentals of Fuel Cells," Nov. 1992.
7. U.S. Department of Energy. "Fuel Cell Bus Program." Nov. 1992.
8. "Energy Partners Restructures, Rolls Out Green Car." *The Hydrogen Letter*, Nov. 1993.
9. Quadfflieg, H. "From Research to Market Application? Experience with the German Hydrogen Fuel Project." *International Journal of Hydrogen Energy*, Vol. 13, No. 6, 1988.
10. Peschka, W. "Hydrogen Combustion in Tomorrow's Energy Technology." *International Journal of Hydrogen Energy*, Vol. 12, No.7, 1987.
11. Furuhama, S. "Hydrogen Engine Technology—R&D at Musashi Institute of Technology." Presented at Hydrogen '91, Symposium presented by the International Association for Hydrogen Energy and the American Academy of Science, September 16-18, 1991.
12. *Electric Vehicle Progress*. March 15, 1993.
13. Struminsky, V. "On the Eve of the Hydrogen Era." 9th World Hydrogen Energy Conference, Paris, June 22-25, 1992.
14. Stewart, Walter F. "Hydrogen as a Vehicular Fuel." in *Recent Developments in Hydrogen Technology, Vol. II*. K.D. Williamson, Jr., and F.J. Edeskuty eds., CRC Press, Boca Raton, Florida.

costs of hydrogen from renewable sources range from about $1 per equivalent gallon of gasoline using large-scale biomass to well over $10 per equivalent gallon using photovoltaic (PV) cells. Of course, final costs to consumers must also reflect transmission and distribution costs and both federal and state taxes. The costs of storing, compressing, and transmitting hydrogen are estimated at $6 to $8 per million Btu, the equivalent of about $0.80 to $1.05 per gallon of gasoline.[158]

Table 2. Present Production Costs of Hydrogen[a]

Source	Hydrogen Cost ($/Million Btu)	Cost of Equivalent Gasoline (Dollars per Gallon)
Natural Gas ($2–4/1000 CF)	5–7	0.65–0.92
Coal	8	1.05
Hydroelectric (Electrolysis)	9–19	1.18–2.49
Wind (Electrolysis)	31	4.06
Solar Thermal (Electrolysis)	37–50	4.85–6.55
Solar PV (Electrolysis)	45–101	5.90–13.23
Biomass (Large scale)	6–10	0.80–1.30

a. Based on Table 3 in "Solar Hydrogen," Ogden, J.M. and J. Nitsch, in *Renewable Energy: Sources for Fuels and Electricity*, Island Press, 1993. Discount rate of 6 percent is assumed.

Economics makes steam reforming the conversion process of choice. Roughly 95 percent of all hydrogen is currently produced from natural gas through this method,[159] in which natural gas and steam react to form carbon dioxide and hydrogen. The price of hydrogen from natural gas depends upon the price of the gas feedstock, the size of the plant, and the borrowing rate for capital. At a 6-percent borrowing rate, hydrogen from a large plant using natural gas costing $2 to $4 per million Btu costs $5 to $7 per million Btu. (In energy terms, this is equivalent to gasoline-production costs of 65 to 92 cents per gallon.) Hydrogen obtained from a large

Box 10. Hydrogen Safety

Does the use of hydrogen pose major safety risks? The highly publicized accidents involving the Challenger space shuttle (1986) and the Hindenburg dirigible (1937) are sometimes cited as proof that the fuel is inherently dangerous. In fact, hydrogen poses greater safety risks than, say, gasoline, in some respects and lower risks in others.[1] Like natural gas, hydrogen is invisible and odorless. Hydrogen flames are invisible and, though extremely hot, radiate little heat, so hydrogen fires can be difficult to locate and extinguish. For these reasons, colorants and odorants would have to be added to hydrogen, even though adding significant amounts would make the fuel less clean. At any rate, additives would have to be picked carefully so the hydrogen wouldn't contaminate the fuel cells.

Hydrogen can be stored safely in many ways, including as metal hydrides, or at very high pressures, as a compressed gas. Tanks for storing natural gas under high pressures, similar to those for storing hydrogen, have proven themselves to be very safe.

Hydrogen can ignite within a rather large range of hydrogen/air mixtures, from 4 to 75 percent (by volume)—the widest

coal-gasification plant would cost about $8 per million Btu (about $1.05 per gallon of gasoline equivalent). Although coal is abundant, major adverse land impacts and much higher emissions of carbon dioxide and other pollutants make natural gas look attractive by comparison.

Table 2 also shows how much it costs to produce hydrogen using electrolysis and various renewable power sources. The cheapest source of electricity would be off-peak hydro power, producing hydrogen at an equivalent gasoline cost of $1.18 to $2.49 per gallon. Hydrogen produced using electricity from wind would cost the equivalent of around $4 per gallon of gasoline. Power from of any common gaseous fuel. However, it is usually the lower limit that is cause for concern, and in this respect hydrogen is similar to natural gas. Compared with gasoline, hydrogen needs very little energy to ignite; on the other hand, hydrogen fires burn themselves out very rapidly. If a hydrogen leak develops, the vapors would disperse quickly, much faster than those of gasoline. Moreover, hydrogen requires a much higher concentration to explode than gasoline or natural gas.

Consumer fears might be tempered by some historical perspective too. In the 1937 Hindenburg disaster, 62 passengers survived and 35 passengers lost their lives. Many who died did so *jumping* from the gondola or from suffering burns and injuries caused by the *diesel* fuel fire, not from the burning hydrogen. Most of the passengers who waited for the airship to land walked away from the accident unharmed.

---

1. Ogden J.M. and J. Nitsch. "Solar Hydrogen." in *Renewable Energy: Sources for Fuels and Electricity*, Island Press, Washington, D.C., 1993; DeLuchi, M.A. "Hydrogen Fuel-Cell Vehicles." Research Report UCD-ITS-92-14, Institute of Transportation Studies, University of California, Davis, Sept. 1992.

PV cells, the most expensive source of hydrogen today, ranges from $6 to $13 per gallon of gasoline equivalent.[a]

In laboratories and pilot projects, hydrogen has been produced by gasifying biomass, such as wood chips or forest and agricultural residues. Projected costs for biomass gasification are $0.80 to $1.11 per equivalent gallon of gasoline.[160] Although biomass plantations have been proposed as large-scale sources of energy,[161] their long-

---

[a] Small experimental PV-hydrogen plants using electrolysis have been constructed in Germany (the Solar-Wasserstoff-Bayern GmbH pilot project) and at Humboldt State University in California.

term sustainability, land and water requirements, and environmental impacts (including soil erosion, fertilizer and pesticide runoff, nutrient loss, and a decline in biodiversity) have yet to be carefully examined.[162]

Per unit of energy, hydrogen costs considerably more than gasoline, but hydrogen vehicles may still be economically competitive with vehicles powered by gasoline or other energy sources. Fuel cells are expected to be two to three times more efficient than gasoline internal combustion engines, so overall fuel requirements on a vehicle-mile basis would be much lower. Also, hydrogen vehicles could be equipped with batteries and regenerative brakes so they could capture some of the vehicle's kinetic energy when they slow down, further increasing overall efficiency. For such reasons, overall life-cycle costs matter far more than simple fuel costs when evaluating the economic feasibility of hydrogen vehicles.

Remaining Technological Hurdles

Hydrogen vehicles won't be commercially attractive until several major technological advances occur.[163] Hydrogen production costs—especially those of using renewable energy sources—will have to fall. Storage technologies will have to improve, and so will the performance of hydrogen fuel-cells. Lastly, a hydrogen-production and -distribution infrastructure will have to be built.

Hydrogen Storage

As is the case with battery-powered electric vehicles, the development of adequate on-board energy storage is a major economic and technological barrier to introducing hydrogen vehicles. Pound for pound, hydrogen has the highest energy density of any common fuel, but it has one of the lowest densities per unit volume. *(See Figures 12 and 13.)* Hydrogen can be stored on board a vehicle in many forms, using radically different technologies—as a gas in high-pressure tanks, as a low-temperature liquid, as a powder in metal hydride tanks, adsorbed to carbon at low temperatures, and in recyclable liquid chemical carriers. Still, none of these options is nearly as simple, compact, or lightweight as gasoline.[164] *(See Box 11.)*

Figure 12. Energy Density of Common Fuels (by weight)

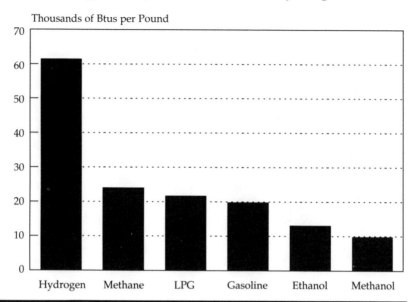

Thousands of Btus per Pound

Fuel Cells

Like a battery, a fuel cell has no moving parts and converts chemical energy into electricity very efficiently. Hydrogen-oxygen fuel cells have a theoretical maximum efficiency of 83 percent,[165] and in practice cells using pure hydrogen and oxygen obtain efficiencies ranging from 50 to 65 percent. Because fuel cells are up to three times as efficient as internal combustion engines, the fuel requirements of a fuel-cell electric vehicle would be far less than those of a similar vehicle equipped with a hydrogen-powered internal combustion engine. Also, unlike batteries, fuel cells don't have to be recharged. They produce electricity as long as the fuel—usually hydrogen—is provided and do so without generating any air pollution.

The basic principles of fuel cells were first set out by Sir William Grove, a British jurist, in 1839.[166] But not until the 1950s

71

Figure 13. Energy Density of Common Fuels (by volume)

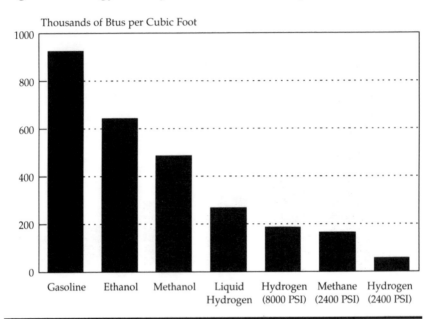

was an alkaline fuel cell built that could generate practical amounts of power over prolonged periods. U.K. scientist Francis Bacon's fuel cells provided the basis for later fuel cell development by Pratt and Whitney, which in turn led to the development of on-board power systems for the Apollo lunar and space-shuttle missions.[167] Fuel cells are now becoming commercially available for both transportation and stationary applications. While fuel-cell power plants with generating capacities up to 11 megawatts have been built and demonstrated, systems for use in motor vehicles are still under development.

Fuel cells are customarily named for their electrolyte. The most advanced fuel cells include phosphoric acid, molten carbonate, solid oxide, solid polymer—also known as the proton exchange membrane (PEM) fuel cell—and alkaline. The most promising fuel cells for transportation applications are phosphoric acid, alkaline, solid oxide, and PEM.[168] *(See Box 12.)*

Life-Cycle Costs of Hydrogen Fuel-Cell Vehicles

Estimating the future costs of buying and operating a hydrogen car is clearly a perilous exercise. Assumptions must be made on the cost and performance of technologies that are currently only prototypes or laboratory projects. But summaries of two preliminary analyses may give some perspective.

In the first, DeLuchi compared the costs in the year 2000 of a 26-mpg, low-emission, high-performance gasoline-powered automobile with electric vehicles powered by batteries (Battery Powered Electric Vehicle, BPEV) and fuel cells.[169] DeLuchi's assumptions were "optimistic but plausible." The fuel-cell electric vehicle (FCEV) was assumed to have a PEM fuel cell, an advanced lithium-disulfide battery to meet peak power needs, and a tank for compressed hydrogen storage. FCEVs would last a third longer than conventional vehicles, accelerate nearly as fast, but have a somewhat shorter range. Major components, such as fuel cells and batteries, would be mass-produced to achieve economies of scale. DeLuchi assumed that gasoline would cost about $1.50 per gallon in 2000 (including all taxes, expressed in 1990 dollars) and that hydrogen would be obtained from either PV cells or biomass sources.

In his base-case scenario, DeLuchi found that FCEVs would have slightly lower life-cycle costs (measured in cents per mile) than the gasoline vehicle even though the purchase price would be higher—whether the hydrogen came from solar cells or biomass. Long-lasting, FCEVs will also be very efficient and inexpensive to maintain. In addition, their range would be only about 250 miles, so on-board hydrogen storage wouldn't need to be extensive. This positive economic profile would be even more favorable if FCEVs' social benefits (no air pollution or greenhouse gas emissions, no imported fuel) were taken into account. As DeLuchi's analysis underscores, neither the vehicle's purchase price nor fuel-production costs are, by themselves, good indicators of the vehicle's overall life-cycle performance.

Mauro of the National Hydrogen Association compared the costs of a 1991 Plymouth Voyager van (with an assumed efficiency of 20 mpg) with those of a FCEV with the same shell and a 300-mile range.[170] Gasoline was assumed to cost $1 per gallon (including

Box 11. Storage Options for Hydrogen

High-Pressure Storage

Storing hydrogen in a high-pressure (3,000 to 10,000 pounds per square inch, psi) tank is a straightforward extension of well-developed technology used to store compressed natural gas. High-pressure hydrogen storage tanks are composite-wound reinforced cylinders with a metal liner and can be refilled in minutes.[1] But this simple storage system is expensive and heavy, which severely restricts vehicle range.

Liquid Hydrogen

Hydrogen can be stored as a liquid at extremely low temperatures (-253°C, -423°F) in highly insulated vacuum containers. A small fraction of the hydrogen, typically 2 to 5 percent, evaporates daily—a potential safety hazard if the vehicle is parked in a garage or other confined area where explosive concentrations could build up. Liquefying hydrogen takes up to 30 percent of the energy of the fuel, making overall storage costs very high. High cost and risk of injury from the cold fluid are both significant drawbacks to using liquid hydrogen in vehicles.

Metal Hydrides

In hydride storage, certain materials absorb hydrogen under moderate pressure (less than 1,000 psi) at low temperatures, forming unstable hydrogen compounds called hydrides. The storage tank contains powdered metals that absorb hydrogen and release heat when the hydrogen is forced into the tank under pressure. The hydrogen is released from the compound when the pressure is reduced and waste heat from the vehicle's engine is applied. On an equal volume basis, hydride tanks store about as much hydrogen as low-temperature liquid systems do. But metal hydride tanks have several disadvantages, including complex heat- and water-management systems, great weight, a long refill-time (20–30 minutes), and high cost.[2]

Carbon Adsorption

In carbon-adsorption storage systems, still very much in the research stage, hydrogen is forced into a refrigerated tank under pressure where it adheres to activated carbon (a highly porous material that adsorbs hydrogen efficiently). A pressure vessel containing carbon-adsorbed hydrogen doesn't differ much from one without carbon: it simply contains more hydrogen and weighs more.[3] The energy density achieved by such systems approaches that of liquid hydrogen and refueling times shouldn't exceed four to five minutes. Carbon adsorption improves greatly as the temperature decreases and could well become the storage means of choice for fuel-cell vehicles if improvements continue.

Sponge Iron

Hydrogen can also be generated directly on board a vehicle. One way under preliminary development is the oxidation (rusting) of iron using steam.[4] In this reaction—once used to produce hydrogen commercially—the oxygen in the steam combines with powdered iron stored in a tank to form rust (iron oxide) and liberates hydrogen in the process. Once the iron is completely converted to iron oxide in the vehicle, either the entire tank can be replaced or the iron oxide can be removed from the tank and replaced with fresh iron—in either case, a matter of minutes. (The iron oxide removed from the vehicle would be converted back to iron for re-use, employing, e.g., renewably generated hydrogen for the reduction process.) Using this system to supply a vehicle with hydrogen would greatly reduce the need for hydrogen pipelines, storage systems, and compressors.

If initial estimates are correct, the weight and volume of the iron needed to power a fuel-cell vehicle would compare with the weight and volume of a tank with hydrogen compressed to 8,000 psi, though the cost for the iron system could be as much as 90 percent lower. For a given vehicle range, the volume of

(continues on next page)

Box 11. *(continued)*

iron needed would be comparable to that of the gasoline in a conventional vehicle. But that amount of iron weighs almost three times as much, and nearly 200 pounds of iron would be needed in a car with a 250-mile range. The amount of iron needed to run the U.S. auto fleet on hydrogen is not large by mining-industry standards, though a vast new iron-reduction infrastructure would have to be created. The New Jersey based H-Power Corporation is studying hydrogen-from-iron systems, but many technical problems remain to be overcome.

Hydrogen Storage Using a Recyclable Liquid Chemical Carrier

In these schemes, hydrogen is carried on board the vehicle as a storable liquid hydrocarbon such as methylcyclohexane ($C_6H_{11}CH_3$ or MCH for short). When MCH, a liquid at normal temperatures and pressures,[5] is heated and passed over a platinum catalyst, hydrogen is liberated and another liquid hydrocarbon (in this case, toluene) is generated. The toluene—whose fumes are about as toxic as petroleum vapors—would be stored in the vehicle's fuel tank and pumped out at the refilling station later. At a central chemical-processing facility, hydrogen would

taxes) and the delivered price of hydrogen was pegged at the equivalent of $2.50 per gallon of gasoline ($20 per million Btu). The FCEV was assumed to have a battery to draw on during acceleration and to store energy from regenerative braking. Mauro assumed that various cost goals would be met for mass-produced FCEV components, including the fuel cell, battery, motors, and controllers. No particular fuel cell was chosen for the analysis; rather, performance goals were used.

Mauro's study indicates that the least expensive FCEV would have a carbon-adsorption storage system and regenerative braking. Even so, the hydrogen vehicle's life-cycle-cost would be about 11 percent higher than that of a gasoline vehicle operating with $1-

be added to the toluene, converting it back to MCH. Such a system would entail fast refueling and reliance on fairly conventional pumps and fuel-storage equipment, but also extra weight, high costs, and the inconvenience associated with cold starting.

1. DeLuchi, M.A. "Hydrogen Fuel-Cell Vehicles." Research Report UCD-ITS-RR-92-14, Institute of Transportation Studies, University of California, Davis, Sept. 1992.

2. DeLuchi, M.A. "Hydrogen Fuel-Cell Vehicles." Research Report UCD-ITS-RR-92-14, Institute of Transportation Studies, University of California, Davis, 1992, Table 3.

3. U.S. Department of Energy, Office of Propulsion Systems. "Feasibility Study of Onboard Hydrogen Storage for Fuel Cells Vehicles, Interim Report." Jan. 1993.

4. Ogden J.M. and J. Nitsch. "Solar Hydrogen," in *Renewable Energy: Sources for Fuels and Electricity*, Island Press, Washington, D.C., 1993; Maceda J.P. and J. Wills. "Advanced Hydrogen Generation and Storage Systems for Fuel Cell Vehicle Support." Presented at the 1992 Windsor Workshop on Alternative Fuels, June 1992; Mayersohn, N.S. "The Outlook for Hydrogen." *Popular Science*, Oct. 1993.

5. Sultan, O. and H. Shaw, Exxon Research and Engineering Company. "Study of Automotive Storage of Hydrogen Using Recyclable Liquid Chemical Carriers." TEC-75-003, prepared for the U.S. Energy Research and Development Administration, June, 1975.

per-gallon gasoline. However, Mauro estimated, environmental damages attributable to producing and consuming gasoline could total an additional $1.12 per gallon. With gas at $2.12 per gallon, the life-cycle cost of the hydrogen van was about 9 percent *below* that of the gasoline van—a calculation consistent with DeLuchi's finding.

These two consistent studies suggest that if today's research-and-development goals for fuel cells and storage technology are met, as they could well be by 2000, FCEVs will be cost-competitive at gasoline prices of about $1.50 per gallon. Cost-competitiveness does not necessarily translate into consumer purchases, however. The initial purchase price of FCEVs could be $8,000 more than for

Box 12. Types of Fuel Cells

Phosphoric Acid Fuel Cells

Phosphoric acid fuel cells (PAFCs) were initially developed in the 1970s to provide electricity and heat at shopping malls, industrial parks, and other large complexes. The most advanced of all fuel-cell technologies, PAFCs have current- and power-densities that are too low to work in transportation applications. Slow start-up (since the cell must be heated to over 200°F), high costs, and excessive weight are also problems. Since phosphoric acid fuel cells are best operated at a constant output, they work best in hybrid systems in which a battery or other device meets the high power-demands of acceleration.[1] Partly because of their weight and size, PAFCs stand their best chance of success in heavy-duty vehicles or locomotives.

Alkaline Fuel Cells

Alkaline fuel cells (AFCs) represent the oldest fuel-cell technology. They were routinely used in space flights and are still used in the space-shuttle program.[2] They have high energy-densities and can start cold. As now designed, alkaline fuel cells require pure hydrogen and pure oxygen free of carbon dioxide. If this restraint could be overcome, alkaline fuel cells could prove suitable for motor vehicle use.[3] Europeans are apparently optimistic on this count since their research efforts have focused on alkaline fuel cells.

Solid Oxide Fuel Cells

Solid oxide fuel cells (SOFCs) have a solid electrolyte. Thus, they last longer than liquid-electrolyte fuel cells[4] and can be built in units as small as five to ten kilowatts. SOFCs operate at high temperatures, typically 1,000°C (1,800°F), so the cells can be used as co-generators to supply both electricity and high-quality waste heat. At high operating temperatures, expensive catalysts are also less necessary and the fuel cells tolerate fuel impurities better. If researchers can bring operating temperatures down to 700°C (1,300°F), the fuel cell's electrical efficiency would rise and manufacturing costs would fall. Lower operating temperatures would also reduce the warm-up period, improving prospects for using the cells in transportation. Although still in the early stages of development, SOFCs hold out the long-term promise of excellent vehicular performance—rugged construction combined with high power and low weight.

Proton Exchange Membrane Fuel Cells

Some analysts consider Proton Exchange Membrane (PEM) fuel cells the most promising fuel-cell technology for use in vehicles.[5] (PEM fuel cells are also called polymer electrolyte fuel cells, solid polymer fuel cells, and solid polymer electrolyte fuel cells.) PEM fuel cells use a proton (a hydrogen ion) conducting membrane—much like kitchen plastic wrap—as their electrolyte. Initially, these membranes were based on polystyrene, but a membrane material called Nafion™, a Teflon™-based product developed by DuPont, performed better and lasted longer. In the mid-1980s, Dow Chemical developed a new polymer for PEM fuel cells permitting higher current- and power-densities.[6]

PEM fuel cells operate at relatively low temperatures (80°C or 180°F), so rapid start-ups are possible at normal outside temperatures. Since low-temperature fuel cells require expensive catalysts (e.g., platinum), researchers are looking for ways to reduce the amount needed. Membrane costs are also very high, and water management within the cell remains a problem. According to DOE researchers, the PEM fuel cell is a promising system for transportation applications, but a major research and development effort is needed to realize this promise.[7] One current research spotlight is on a PEM fuel cell that can run on methanol (CH_3OH) broken down on board the vehicle to supply hydrogen and carbon monoxide.

(continues on next page)

Box 12. *(continued)*

1. U.S. Department of Energy. "Phosphoric Acid Fuel Cells." Nov. 1992.
2. Mauro, R.L. "The Technology Assessment of Hydrogen Vehicles, A Report for the National Renewable Energy Laboratory by the National Hydrogen Association." Washington, D.C., June 1992.
3. U.S. Department of Energy. "Principles of Fuel Cell Operation." Nov. 1992.
4. Goldstein, R. "Solid Oxide Fuel Cell Development." *EPRI Journal*, Oct./Nov. 1992.
5. Swan, D.H. and A.J. Appleby, "Fuel Cells and Other Long Range Technology Options for Electric Vehicles: Knowledge Gaps and Development Priorities." in *The Urban Electric Vehicle*, Proceedings of an International Conference, Stockholm, Sweden, May 25–27, 1992. OECD Document.
6. U.S. Department of Energy. "Proton-Exchange Membrane (PEM) Fuel Cells." Nov. 1992.
7. Patil, P.G. et al. "U.S. Research and Development Program on Fuel Cells for Transportation Applications." EVS-11, 1990.

a conventional vehicle, according to DeLuchi.[171] (As mentioned earlier, anyone shopping for battery-powered EVs would get a similar sticker shock.)

American consumers find it hard to make investments that make eminently good sense from an economic and national perspective if they have to pay more up front. Clearly, the task for policy-makers is to dismantle this barrier through education, regulation, innovative financing mechanisms (e.g., leasing arrangements), or economic measures—such as higher gasoline taxes or tax credits. But since such changes can't happen overnight, the widespread use of hydrogen vehicles seems a few decades away.

IV.

Impacts of Zero-Emission Vehicles

If large numbers of zero emission vehicles are introduced in the United States, oil consumption, air pollution, and greenhouse gas emissions will all drop. Yet, the power plants used to recharge the batteries or produce the hydrogen will still emit some pollution, and decision-makers need at least rough estimates of the security- and air-quality impacts and the global warming benefits that could be realized by beginning a shift to electrically powered vehicles. They also need to know how an EV-based transportation system might affect electric utilities.

Curbing Air Pollution

Numerous analysts have compared the air-pollution and greenhouse-gas emissions of battery-powered vehicles with those of conventional vehicles.[172] In one detailed study, University of California researchers examined the impact of introducing electric cars and vans on emissions of hydrocarbons (HC), nitrogen oxides (NO_x), carbon monoxide (CO), particulate matter (PM), and sulfur oxides (SO_x) in the year 2010.[173] The authors assumed that gasoline vehicles met stringent emission controls, burned low-volatility gasoline, and were subject to tough inspection and maintenance programs. They further assumed an electricity generation mix of about 68 percent fossil fuel and 32 percent non-fossil (nuclear, hydro, solar), about the same as today. The fossil-fueled plants—half of them coal-fired—were assumed to have "moderate" pollution controls.

The California team concluded that (on a grams-of-pollution per mile basis) battery-powered EVs would virtually eliminate HC and CO emissions and cut NO_x emissions by 60 percent. Although particulate and sulfur oxide emissions would increase with EVs, the overall contribution of cars and vans would be relatively minor in either case since together they account for only about 11 percent of national particulate emissions and about 1 percent of sulfur oxide emissions.[174] (If the coal plants projected in this scenario were replaced with natural-gas-fired steam plants, sulfur oxide and particulate emissions would also drop dramatically.) Moreover, since total national sulfur-dioxide emissions are capped by the Clean Air Act, in practice there will be no net increase in these emissions at all. (Utilities will be required to use either lower-sulfur fuels or appropriate scrubbing technology to keep their sulfur emissions below the cap imposed by the Clean Air Act Amendments.)

Another study, carried out by the Washington-based think-tank, Resources for the Future, examined the impacts on Los Angeles air quality in the year 2010 of introducing electric vehicles.[175] The researchers assumed that new gasoline-powered vehicles would meet California's tough 1997 emissions standards and that new electric power plants would employ the most effective controls for nitrogen oxides. If so, the authors concluded, introducing EVs into the vehicle mix of Los Angeles would significantly reduce emissions of hydrocarbons, carbon monoxide, nitrogen oxides, and benzene, irrespective of how and where the electricity for charging the batteries is generated. Specifically, if the fleet were 15 percent EVs and all new power plants were located outside of Los Angeles, total hydrocarbons emissions in the basin would be cut by about 9 percent, nitrogen-oxide emissions by 12 percent, sulfur dioxide by 10 percent, and carbon monoxide by 24 percent. Introducing EVs in other U.S. urban areas would also improve air quality, the researchers contend.

In California, the Air Resources Board has concluded that, if emissions from power plants are taken into account, EV emissions are substantially lower than those from ultra-low-emission vehicles (ULEV).[176] One reason is that emission-control systems on gasoline-powered vehicles gradually deteriorate as they age. Another is that most of the electric power plants serving California rely on natural gas, by far the cleanest fossil fuel.

In yet another study, researchers quantified the air-quality impacts of introducing electric vehicles in the northeastern states.[177] Allowing for deterioration in performance, the authors compared carbon dioxide and other emissions from gasoline vehicles meeting the new Tier I federal emissions standards with those of electric vehicles charged by the expected regional fuel mix. Per vehicle-mile traveled, EVs would cut VOC and CO emissions by more than 99 percent, and NO_x emissions by about 70 percent. Sulfur emissions would be expected to increase but, as noted, total emissions are capped by the Clean Air Act.

Cutting Oil Imports

For several reasons, electric vehicles will reduce national security risks by cutting the need to import oil. First, cars and trucks account for more than half of U.S. oil demand, and DOE projects motor-vehicle oil consumption to increase by two thirds between 1990 and 2030. *(See Figure 14.)* The larger the share of the nation's oil demand vehicles account for, the greater the opportunity for cutting oil use. Second, very little of the oil Americans consume—less than 4 percent—is used to generate electricity, and most of that is needed during daytime peak periods. As a result, using off-peak electricity to charge electric vehicles will have the effect of substituting coal, natural gas, and other fuels for oil, reducing national oil consumption.

Projecting how much oil EVs might displace requires making assumptions about the number and average fuel use of the conventional vehicles that electric vehicles will replace. Obviously, estimating how many EVs will be introduced in the coming years is a tricky business. For one thing, state decision-makers or court challenges could topple the clean-air regulations that mandate the introduction of these vehicles in California and a number of northeastern states. Or fuel prices could fall if OPEC decided to undermine the competitiveness of new, non-petroleum energy technologies. On the other hand, a breakthrough in battery or flywheel technologies or a major reduction in manufacturing costs could make EVs much more attractive to consumers. So could a price spike in gasoline in the wake of another upheaval in the Persian

Figure 14. Trends in Motor Vehicle Oil Demand (Reference Case)

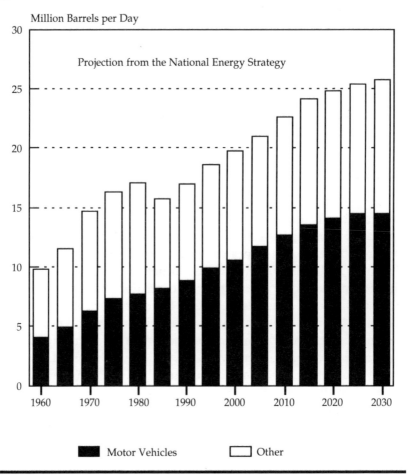

Gulf, a resurgence in control over world oil prices by OPEC, or changes in domestic fuel taxes. It is also possible that in the coming decade, global warming symptoms could suddenly become more threatening, forcing a rapid reduction in world fossil-fuel consumption, much as the phase-out of CFCs was accelerated when the ozone hole over Antarctica was discovered.

Still, explicit assumptions have to be made or EV growth can't be projected. *(See Box 13.)* As an upper limit, the estimate used here is that by 2003 up to 1.4 million EVs could be on the road nationwide, less than 1 percent of the total fleet. But if the rapid growth projected during the coming decade were to continue, by the year 2010 there could be 14 million EVs on the road.

Because battery performance limits the range of EVs, they are likely to be used initially in urban areas for commuting, deliveries, and other short trips—not an insurmountable problem since the average trip is only 9 miles long.[178] If the gasoline-powered vehicles displaced have an average city-driving fuel efficiency of 25 mpg and are driven 30 miles per day (11,000 miles per year), the oil savings—including those from refinery and transportation losses[179]—would total about 13 barrels of oil (about 526 gallons of oil) per year for each EV introduced. If most EVs are recharged at night, when very little oil is used for power generation, oil savings from introducing EVs would be about 14 thousand barrels per day by the year 2000, a modest amount indeed. *(See Figure 15.)* But by the year 2010, the total could grow to half a million barrels per day, about 7 percent of today's imports and about 3 percent of imports as projected by the Department of Energy. If EV use continued to grow rapidly, oil imports would drop commensurately.

Alleviating Global Warming

How much carbon-dioxide emissions can be reduced by replacing internal combustion engine vehicles with comparable battery-powered electric vehicles will depend on the relative efficiencies of the vehicles and the nature and amounts of emissions from the electric power plants used to recharge the EVs.[a] But if gasoline-powered vehicles are compared with EVs manufactured from the same body—so-called "EV conversions"—a reasonable estimate can be made.

---

[a] Carbon dioxide is by far the most important greenhouse gas contributing to global warming. While motor vehicles also contribute to increasing concentrations of nitrous oxide, CFCs, tropospheric ozone, and methane we will limit our discussion here to CO_2.

Box 13. Projecting the Growth in EVs

To project the number of electric vehicles that will be on the road over the next two decades, we assume that California and the 12 northeastern states, plus the District of Columbia, will implement California's Low Emission Vehicle program. These regulations require automakers to introduce Zero Emission Vehicles (ZEVs) beginning in 1998—which, for now, means introducing electric vehicles. The ZEV regulations require that 2 percent of new light-duty vehicles (those weighing less than 6,000 pounds) be emission-free in 1998, rising to 5 percent in 2001 and 10 percent in 2003. These requirements are extrapolated for intermediate years, and the assumption here is that growth of 1.5 percent per year in the number of new vehicles will continue. Given these assumptions, by 2003 upwards of 460,000 new EVs could be registered annually nationwide— about 3 percent of all new light-duty vehicles nationally—with a total of 1.4 million EVs on the road in California and the northeastern states.

To extend this projection to the year 2010, we assume that growth in EV sales—considered as a percentage of new motor vehicles sales—can be approximated with an "S" shaped (logistic) curve. The spread of many technological innovations, (including automatic transmissions, air conditioners, power steering, disc brakes, and even the substitution of motor vehicles for horse-drawn vehicles) follows this curve, as Nakicenovic has shown.[1] Figure 16 shows a logistic curve fit to the projected growth in new-vehicle sales. If EV growth does follow this pattern, close to 25 percent of new light-duty vehicles would be electric by the year 2010. By then, new electric vehi-

---

First, consider Chrysler's gasoline-powered minivan, sold as the Dodge Caravan and the Plymouth Voyager. As a gasoline-powered vehicle, this minivan, equipped with the 3-liter engine and the 4-speed automatic transmission, has an EPA-estimated fuel efficiency of about 18 mpg in city driving. (Its electric counterpart, incles would number about 3.6 million annually and more than 14 million would be on the road. *(See Figure 17.)*

The growth in new EV production implied by Figure 17 is enormous, averaging about 33 percent per year between 2004 and 2010. Is such rapid growth feasible? Yes. In fact, very high early growth rates are common with many new technologies, both automotive and otherwise. For instance, between 1900 and 1917 the motor vehicle share of the road-vehicle fleet rose from 1 percent to 50 percent.[2] By 1930, motor vehicles had captured virtually the entire road-vehicle market from animals. Similarly, the introduction of cellular phones grew (1986–1989) at almost 60 percent per year, compact disks (1985-1989) at 29 percent, auto security systems (1986–1989) at 25 percent, telephone-answering equipment (1985–1989) at 38 percent, and personal computers (1981–1988), at 36 percent.[3] Since EVs are in many ways simpler to manufacture than internal combustion cars and vehicle design would not change much, the growth projected in Figure 17 would certainly seem technically possible.

Of course, no one can guarantee that the rapid EV growth projected in Figure 17 will occur. How fast these vehicles are introduced will depend on many factors—among them, oil prices, technological improvements in energy storage, environmental developments, and state and federal government policies.

---

1. Nakicenovic, N. "The Automobile Road to Technological Change, Diffusion of the Automobile as a Process of Technological Substitution." *Technological Forecasting and Social Change 29*, 309–40, 1986.

2. Nakicenovic, N. "The Automobile Road to Technological Change, Diffusion of the Automobile as a Process of Technological Substitution." *Technological Forecasting and Social Change 29*, 309–40, 1986.

3. U.S. Statistical Abstract, 1992, Tables 1279 and 1274.

troduced commercially as the Dodge Caravan Electric, would be used mostly in city driving, so urban fuel efficiency is an appropriate basis for comparison.) The electric minivan is now available for commercial testing, mostly by electric utilities. Equipped with a nickel-iron battery expected to last 100,000 miles, regenerative

Figure 15. Oil Displaced by Electric Vehicles

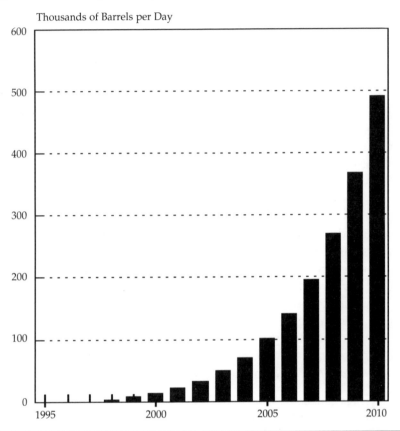

Thousands of Barrels per Day

braking, and power brakes and steering, the Dodge Caravan Electric accelerates to 50 mph in 14 seconds, has a top speed of 65 mph, and a range of about 120 miles. Its energy consumption, measured on the urban portion of the federal driving cycle, is 0.44 kw-hrs per mile, as measured at the wall outlet.[180]

The second EV considered here is the Geo Metro and its electric version, the Force, an EV conversion marketed by Solectria. The energy consumption of these very similar vehicles was carefully measured in urban driving tests by Southern California Edison

Figure 16. Projection of EV Share of U.S. Motor Vehicle Sales

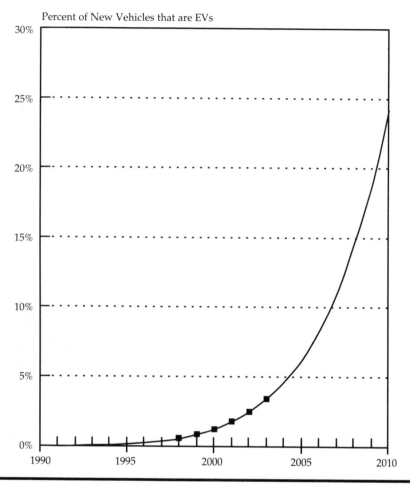

Company,[181] which pegged the fuel efficiency of the Geo Metro in city driving at 39.1 mpg and found that the Force consumed about 0.21 kw-hrs per mile over the same course.

The third vehicle is a 1991 Honda CRX HF, a very efficient two-seater that in city driving gets between 43 and 49 mpg (as estimated by EPA), depending on emission controls and fuel system differences. This car was converted to an electric vehicle by AC

Figure 17. Projected Growth in the Number of Electric Vehicles

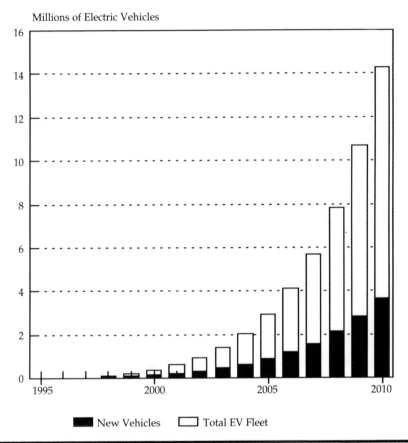

Millions of Electric Vehicles

■ New Vehicles   ☐ Total EV Fleet

Propulsion, a California-based research and development firm. In the urban portion of the federal FUDS test cycle, the car consumed a mere 0.155 kw-hrs per mile, as measured by the California Air Resources Board.

The corresponding efficiencies of these three vehicles as gasoline and EV conversions are shown in Figure 18. Using this information, it is easy to calculate the carbon dioxide emissions resulting from driving each of these six vehicles for 100 urban miles. For the gasoline versions, the energy losses in refining and transport-

Figure 18. Efficiencies of EVs Compared with Their Gasoline Versions

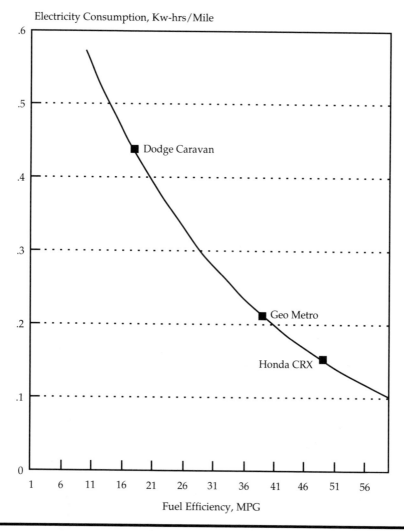

Electricity Consumption, Kw-hrs/Mile

ing the petroleum were included. For all EVs, various generating mixes (including the present national mix of 55-percent coal, 9-percent natural gas, 4-percent oil, with the rest hydro and nuclear; an all-coal mix; an all-natural gas mix; and an all-solar or nuclear system with presumed near-zero CO_2 emissions) were considered. The mining and processing of fuels, as well as electrical transmission losses were also taken into account.

Figure 19 shows the resulting carbon dioxide emissions. As the Figure indicates, recharging the electric vehicles using coal-fired power plants would result in carbon-dioxide emissions 17 to 22

Figure 19. Reductions in CO_2 Emissions from Converting
Gasoline Vehicles to EVs (for various power sources)

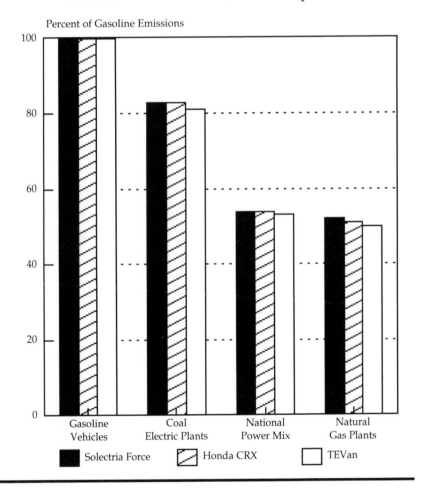

percent less than those of the corresponding gasoline versions. With today's national electrical power mix—which includes both nuclear and hydro capacity—EV emissions would be 46 to 49 percent less; if recharged by natural gas power plants—the likely source in many locations—48 to 52 percent less; if recharged by nuclear, hydro, or solar plants, carbon-dioxide emissions would fall to virtually zero. As these simple estimates suggest, no matter what the mix of generating plants, in city driving using battery-powered versions of these paired vehicles, EVs would bring carbon-dioxide emissions down far below what they would be with gasoline-powered vehicles.

What assumptions about the total amount of carbon dioxide displaced by EVs are plausible? First, the national electrical generating mix will not change appreciably from what it is today. Second, the projected growth in EVs will occur as described in the box. And, third, the annual oil consumption per gasoline-powered vehicle displaced (a 25-mpg vehicle driven 30 miles per day) is 527 gallons per year. Under these assumptions, the gasoline-powered vehicle would release about 1.3 metric tons of carbon per year and an EV recharged using either natural gas plants or the present national mix would cut these emissions by about half (some 0.6 metric tons of carbon per vehicle). In 2003, if there were 1.4 million EVs on the road, carbon-dioxide emissions would drop by about 835 thousand tons of carbon below what they would be if no EVs were introduced. By 2010, emissions would be cut by ten times this amount, some 8.3 million metric tons of carbon. For perspective here, U.S. carbon dioxide emissions in 1990 totaled about 1.4 billion metric tons of carbon.[182] Clearly, reducing carbon-dioxide emissions by substituting one technology for another and sticking with the existing fuel mix for generating electricity will take a long time: even by 2010, less than 1 percent of present total carbon-dioxide emissions would be cut by using battery EVs.

The Costs and Benefits of EVs in Mitigating National Problems

How do electric vehicles compare, in economic terms, with other options for addressing air pollution, national energy-security

93

concerns, and climate change? This question is difficult to answer. Many technological uncertainties make economic analysis difficult. Who can speak with confidence about when advances in batteries, flywheels, fuel cells, and hydrogen storage will occur? About how oil prices will change in the next decade? About the pace of global climate change? Or other potentially important factors affecting the net costs of owning and operating EVs?

Ideally, the additional costs of alternative measures that would achieve the same national goals should be compared. But electric vehicles confer multiple benefits, as do some of the alternative options for reducing the social costs of our current reliance on oil-powered vehicles. For example, EV use would reduce air pollution and carbon-dioxide emissions while the use of reformulated gasoline would help with the first but not the second. Similarly, comparing the costs of reducing VOCs by introducing EVs to the costs of inspection and maintenance programs would ignore the climate-related and oil-reduction benefits of using EVs.

Given these methodological problems, can it be determined whether the additional benefits of electric vehicles justify their additional costs? Since applying a formal cost-effectiveness or cost-benefit test to electric vehicles is so intrinsically difficult, a simpler approach may make more sense: comparing the additional costs of owning and operating electric vehicles to the estimated costs of achieving similar benefits using alternative approaches. Such calculations will never reveal whether the additional costs of electric vehicles are more or less than the value of the associated benefits or whether EVs are more or less costly compared to all other means of producing similar benefits. But they do provide a rough answer to the question of whether EVs are in the same economic ballpark as other options that society seems willing to consider to achieve national goals.

The extra cost of electric vehicles can be calculated using the analysis presented above on the relative costs of Chrysler's gasoline-powered minivan and its electric counterpart, the Caravan Electric. In brief, the assumptions are that the performance and cost goals for advanced batteries would be met and that gasoline would continue to sell for about $1.20 per gallon, while the findings are that the EV would cost about $240 more annually to own and run than its gasoline counterpart.[a] It is this $240 annual premium that van owners would pay for the benefits that come with using Chrysler's Caravan Electric.

Cutting Air Pollution

EVs will cut VOC and CO emissions to negligible levels and greatly reduce NO_x emissions, all important contributors to the formation of urban smog. The amount by which VOCs—in many areas of the country, the key ingredient in ozone formation— would be reduced by replacing a new gas-powered vehicle with an EV can be estimated by using the new federal Tier I emission standard for gasoline vehicles and allowing for some deterioration over the life of the car.[183] Assuming average lifetime VOC emissions of 0.597 grams per mile, driving an EV would keep about 13 pounds of VOCs (as well as 185 pounds of carbon monoxide) out of the air each year. Typical costs for VOC-reduction measures (reducing fuel volatility, enhancing vehicle inspection and maintenance, capturing vapors from gas-station pumps) range from $1,000 to $5,000 per ton of VOCs removed.[184] According to one recent analysis, gasoline taxes could reduce VOC emissions for less than $1,000 a ton in some areas.[185] If an average of $3,000 per ton is assumed, the value of avoiding 13 pounds of VOCs through EV use would be about $20 per year. At $1,000 per ton, the value would fall to $6.50 per year.

Reducing Oil Imports

How much is it worth to the United States to reduce oil imports (currently about 41 percent of supply)? Motor vehicles now account for over half of U.S. oil consumption, and the U.S. transportation system (including planes and ships) depends almost totally on oil, ever more of it imported. The savings from introducing a Chrysler Caravan Electric—including savings from refinery and transportation losses—would be about 16 barrels (about 667 gal-

---

[a] While this $240 value is the correct one to use in making national cost-effectiveness estimates, it is not the actual extra premium that would be seen by consumers. The federal 10-percent tax credit on EVs would reduce electric vehicle costs to about $100 per year less than those of the gasoline car.

lons) of oil per year for each van introduced (assuming that no oil-generated electricity is used for recharging).

The United States' growing dependence on imported oil, particularly from the politically unstable Persian Gulf, can impose several kinds of costs on U.S. society, but such costs are extremely difficult to gauge accurately. Some analysts argue that the costs of mitigation measures are a useful approximation of the overall risks. For example, the military costs of protecting the vast oil resources of the Persian Gulf—estimated by the Cato Institute at roughly $50 billion per year during peacetime[a]—are one such measure.[186] In another study, national security expenditures for U.S. oil imports are estimated at $11 per barrel of imported oil (in 1992 dollars).[187] These military expenditures can be viewed as a mitigation strategy to reduce the risks of disruptions and interventions.

Currently, the U.S. public pays these military expenditures—which may or may not accurately reflect the actual economic costs being imposed on U.S. security—through general tax revenues. Should oil consumers pay the bill instead? There are several arguments against such an approach. First, protecting Persian Gulf oil resources may not be the only reason for a military presence in the Middle East, and, even if the United States significantly reduced its own oil imports, it might still feel a need to protect this region. According to this reasoning, oil consumers should not have to foot the entire bill for military expenditures. (All oil-importing nations, including the Europeans and the Japanese, benefit when the United States safeguards access to Middle Eastern oil supplies, a fact not lost on the countries that pitched in to pay for the war with Iraq in 1991.)

There are other ways to reduce the risks of importing oil, such as increasing the fuel efficiency of new motor vehicles. Characteristic costs for cutting oil (gasoline) use in vehicles through improved efficiency range from $20 to $30 per barrel (48 to 71 cents per gallon of saved gasoline).[188] There may be less expensive alternatives that would reduce oil consumption, such as a gasoline tax.

---

[a] This sum reflects the costs of supporting the so-called Central Command and of maintaining four land divisions, nine tactical air wings, and three navy air-craft-carrier battle groups; it does not include the estimated $5 billion per year of a conventional war.

More formal economic assessments of the security risks of oil imports suggest lower costs. Over the last twenty years, estimates of oil-import costs have ranged from $10 to over $40 per barrel.[189] More recent analyses, however, suggest costs in the low end of the range, perhaps well below $10 a barrel. Bohi and Toman, for example, identify only two categories of costs associated with oil imports—the potential consequences of exporting nations to exercise non-competitive market power, and the economic impacts of oil-price variability under a system of rigid or inflexible wages and prices.[190] While the authors assign no specific dollar value to these costs, they do suggest that such costs may be large enough to warrant policy responses, including R&D spending on energy supply alternatives, oil price stabilization initiatives, or oil consumption taxes. Nevertheless, the authors believe that the true costs are likely to be lower than earlier estimates.

Taken together, these analyses suggest that the costs of U.S. reliance on imported oil will continue to be the subject of debate that is likely to grow as the United States imports more of its supply over the coming years. To reflect the many uncertainties, a range of estimates is used to assess the benefit of reducing oil imports. If $25-per-barrel is saved from efficiency improvements, the 16 imported barrels saved per year have a value of about $400. At $8 per barrel, the benefit would be worth $128.

Reducing CO_2 Emissions

If EVs are recharged using natural gas plants or the present national mix of electrical power sources—which includes both nuclear and hydro capacity—their CO_2 emissions would be about half those of a comparable gasoline vehicle. Over a year, carbon emissions from a gasoline-powered Caravan driven 10,000 city miles total about 3,500 pounds (about 1.6 metric tons). How much this carbon discharge actually costs society defies straightforward analysis, but mitigation costs can be estimated even though they vary greatly depending on which approach is taken.[191] Some investments in end-use efficiency (those in lighting improvements, for instance) can reduce carbon-dioxide emissions at considerable economic savings. As further CO_2 reductions are required, the costs of various conservation and substitution measures increase.

Net costs of efficiency improvements can reach $20 per metric ton of carbon emissions reduced; those of improving electric generation efficiency can exceed $40 per metric ton. If a value of $30 per ton of carbon is assumed, the van's reduction of carbon-dioxide emissions by 0.8 tons has a value of $24.

Together, the benefits of reduced VOC emissions, lowered oil imports, and reduced carbon dioxide emissions are worth from $158 to over $444 per year. At the upper end of this range, the benefits are worth almost twice the extra cost ($240) of owning and operating the EV. At the lower end, the additional EV costs are about 50 percent greater than the value of the benefits. Thus, if research-and-development goals for EVs are achieved and fuel prices stay low, switching to battery-powered electric vehicles could be an economically rational way to reduce smog and carbon monoxide, cut oil imports, and reduce carbon-dioxide emissions.

Impacts on Utilities

If the number of EVs grows rapidly, electric utilities could be affected dramatically. Higher kw-hr sales, increased peak demands, and a decrease in the quality of the electric power available from the grid are all possibilities.

The quantity of electricity consumed by electric vehicles depends mainly on how efficient they are and how far they are driven. Typical prototype light-duty electric vehicles consume 0.2 to 0.5 kw-hrs for each mile driven. Driven 30 miles per day (the national average for passenger cars), an electric vehicle would need a daily charge of 6 to 15 kw-hrs and annual consumption would range from 2,200 to 5,500 kw-hrs. Since average consumption per U.S. household is about 10,000 kw-hrs per year, an electric vehicle could increase a family's electricity consumption by 22 to 55 percent.

If most people recharge their EVs during the day, peak loads will increase, utilities will have to add new generating capacity, and smog benefits will be less than during night-time charging. For instance, Southern California Edison Company estimates that if 200,000 or more EVs are recharged largely during daytime, the utility will have to add new generating capacity.[192] The utility could handle about seven times this number of EVs if they were recharged at night.

The amount of time needed to recharge EVs will also have a major impact on utilities. If it takes ten hours overnight, average power demand would be only 0.5 to 1.5 kilowatts (kws), easily managed by today's electric power distribution systems. But fast recharging over, say, 10 to 20 minutes, would be a different matter, imposing a power demand of 60 to 150 kws on the distribution system. If most people opted for the fast recharge, the utility's distribution system would have to be upgraded at major expense.

To avoid having to build new capacity or rebuild transmission and distribution systems—both of which would increase consumer costs—utilities should encourage EV owners to recharge their electric vehicles slowly overnight by introducing "time-of-use" electric rates. These would be lowest for slow, overnight recharging that imposes only a modest load. For peak periods or high charging loads, much higher electric rates would apply.

As utilities, automakers, local governments, and industry lay plans for introducing EVs, the natural tendency is to make EV recharging convenient for consumers, allowing EV drivers to recharge their vehicles at virtually any available parking space. But while recharging stations at work, parking lots, malls, and restaurants may seem like a good way to give electric vehicles greater range, utilities and their customers could end up paying a steep price. If publicly accessible recharging facilities are made widely available to speed the introduction of EVs, EV users should be charged the full cost of power provided during peak periods—in general a fairly high electricity price—especially for quick recharging. Underpricing peak-load power will only encourage EV drivers to add to peakloads, thus imposing costly burdens on utilities and their customers.

Besides minimizing power costs, recharging at night would also minimize smog formation from utility nitrogen oxide emissions. Smog (ozone) needs sunlight to form, and the air pollutants from utility stacks would have long dispersed by morning.

There are two exceptions to the rule of encouraging only nighttime recharging. The first would be when the power is derived from solar technologies (such as photovoltaic cells) that provide

99

their peak power output around solar noon. *(See Box 14.)* The second would be recharging from local electrical storage systems (say, batteries or flywheels) that are themselves charged during off-peak periods or by solar sources.

Utilities have cause to worry about other EV impacts too. One is the effect that widespread battery recharging could have on the quality of power from the grid. Poorly designed charging systems could introduce electrical "noise" into the grid, with subsequent impacts on the performance of other electrical devices such as computers—a potential problem being addressed by an Infrastructure Working Committee organized by the utility industry. Another concern of both utilities and automakers is the possible link between strong electromagnetic fields (EMF) and various forms of cancer. The use of virtually any kind of electrical equipment—from electric blankets and toasters to high-voltage transmission lines—creates these fields, and the possibility that exposure to low levels of EMFs could increase the risk of cancer has been known for some time.[193] (One recent Swedish study apparently confirms the link.[194]) Of course, gasoline-powered vehicles also have many electrical devices that produce EMFs, and one recent study measuring EMFs in both EVs and conventional vehicles found that the fields were comparable, and very small in both cases.[195] Even so, measures to reduce EMFs in EVs are under study by the Department of Energy, the National Institute of Environmental Health Sciences, and the Electric Power Research Institute.

* * *

Without doubt, a program to aggressively introduce electric vehicles would enhance national security and local air quality while reducing national carbon-dioxide emissions. For the first decade or two, the impacts would not be large. But they would become increasingly significant as the fraction of EVs in the total fleet grew. The environmental benefits—reduction in smog and carbon-dioxide emissions—could increase even more quickly if the nation phases in the use of renewable sources of electricity and hydrogen, such as wind and photovoltaics.

Careful planning is needed to avoid unwanted effects. Time-of-day pricing will be essential if utilities are to meet the heavy power demands. Potential health risks from electromagnetic fields and

Box 14. Solar Recharging in Sacramento and Tampa

The Sacramento Municipal Utility District (SMUD) and the University of South Florida at Tampa have both constructed experimental PV-powered recharging systems for EVs.[1] The SMUD station is powered by solar panels with a peak output of 12 kilowatts that is capable of generating, on average, about 68 kw-hrs per day. The facility can recharge up to 16 EVs at a time—over 4 kw-hrs per electric vehicle each day. The Florida facility can charge the vehicle batteries directly or it can charge on-site batteries, which in turn can be used to recharge vehicle batteries at night. The 20 kilowatts (peak) of PV cells can also supply AC power to the grid.

Can PV recharging centers really meet a significant portion of EV needs? Yes, and a simple calculation shows why. Suppose a commuter drives her EV to work 20 miles one-way. A highly efficient EV—such as the Solectria Force—would consume about 0.2 kw-hrs per mile, so she would use about 4 kw-hrs for the one-way trip, well within the capability of the PV recharging station. Since a square meter of solar cells (with a 15-percent efficiency) will produce about 0.8 kw-hr of electricity per day, 15 square meters (about 160 square feet) of PV cells would, on average, provide 12 kw-hrs, more than enough to recharge the EV. This area is comparable to the parking area occupied by the vehicle itself. In short, the PVs on the roof of the parking space should be able to recharge the vehicle over the course of the day for the entire round trip from work to home and return. Interestingly, the cost of the electricity from PV cells today (a hefty 25 cents per kw-hr delivered) would be about the same, per vehicle-mile traveled, as the cost of gasoline, about four to five cents per mile. (PV costs are expected to continue falling as efficiencies improve and larger, automated manufacturing facilities are built.)

---

1. "EV Charging Station Opened to the Public in Sacramento." *Electric Vehicle Progress*, October 1, 1992; Stefanakos, E. "Driving With the Sun: PV Electric Vehicle Recharging Station." *Solar Today*, Jan./Feb. 1993.

toxic wastes from used batteries will have to be addressed systematically through legal or economic incentives to return spent batteries. As for significant extra national costs in introducing these vehicles, the jury is still out, and the verdict depends largely on the future price of petroleum, on the one hand, and the success in developing new electricity storage and hydrogen technology on the other. The analysis presented here, however, suggests that EVs—whether powered by batteries or fuel cells—would be cost competitive if the social and environmental costs of oil-powered vehicles were fully reflected in their prices.

V.

SUMMARY AND POLICY RECOMMENDATIONS

Persistent U.S. environmental, security, and economic problems stem in part from heavy reliance on oil-powered motor vehicles. Over the past twenty years, continued engineering improvements have reduced new-vehicle pollution emissions and improved fuel efficiency. Yet, for several reasons, the problems endure. The relentless growth in the number and use of internal combustion engine vehicles has overwhelmed efforts to reduce fuel consumption. And pollution-control devices on cars and trucks deteriorate over time.

Reducing the fuel-related threats posed by motor vehicles will require the gradual substitution of zero emission vehicles (ZEVs) for internal combustion vehicles over the next few decades. Such an approach will have both short- and long-term elements. In the next few years, few ZEVs can be put on the road and U.S. policy should emphasize improving new-vehicle fuel efficiency, further reducing emissions from the present fleet, and cutting the number of vehicle-miles traveled. Key here are higher fuel prices (to reflect unpaid social and environmental costs), introducing reformulated gasoline to cut pollution emissions, and a continuation of inspection and maintenance programs, supplemented with the use of roadside instruments that can identify high-polluting vehicles.[196]

In the longer term, ZEVs will have to be phased in, powered by sustainable sources of energy—including wind, solar power, or hydrogen derived from renewable sources. A ZEV will emit much less pollution and carbon dioxide than even the cleanest internal combustion engine. According to CARB's Tom Cackette, "ZEVs have no tailpipe emissions to deteriorate—zero will always be zero. They also emit no toxic emissions, and have substantially lower carbon dioxide emissions than conventional vehicles."[197]

The transition to ZEVs will take three to four decades. For at least the next ten years, zero emission vehicles will mean battery-powered vehicles.[a] Ultimately, ZEVs will be powered by some combination of batteries, hydrogen fuel cells, flywheels, and ultracapacitors.

Electric vehicles will help the United States make the inevitable, long-term transition to reliance on sustainable energy sources. Sizable benefits could be realized within 20 years if these new technologies were phased in aggressively. Moreover, if current goals for performance and cost can be met, these benefits could be achieved for about what the nation seems willing to pay to achieve the same results using other means.

Realizing the benefits of ZEVs will require an integrated national effort on many fronts. Making gasoline prices more accurately reflect the full social costs of burning oil is an indispensable step in improving the economic attractiveness of zero-emission vehicles. Also needed is more broadly based research on advanced technologies, along with user-friendly facilities for vehicle refueling, new fleet-purchase programs, and other incentives to help establish markets and bring down initial consumer costs. Some of these initiatives will best be undertaken at the federal level; others are more suited to state and local action. Some are already authorized by federal legislation and need only be funded and implemented.

Reforming Fuel Prices

One of the most important single actions that could be taken to accelerate the introduction of zero-emission vehicles would be to reform the pricing of gasoline and diesel fuel. Even though the

---

[a] Under some circumstances, CARB has indicated, it might certify hybrid electric vehicles as ZEVs, but their on-board power generators would most likely not burn a volatile liquid fuel such as gasoline or methanol mixtures. To be certified as ZEVs, hybrids would probably use gas turbines or fuel cells to recharge the batteries.

seemingly straightforward move of raising fuel taxes is in practice fraught with political and conceptual difficulties, these costs are real and ought to be reflected, however imperfectly, in the price of fuel at the pump. According to one rough estimate, U.S. motor vehicle drivers impose nearly $300 billion per year more in costs on society than they pay directly themselves.[198] Of these, some $70 billion are related to air pollution, climate change, imports, and noise—all products of oil combustion. This translates to about $0.50 for every gallon of gasoline and diesel fuel consumed by American cars, trucks, and buses, and several researchers have concluded that increasing fuel prices by about this amount would be enough to make advanced-battery and fuel-cell powered vehicles cost-competitive with oil-powered vehicles on a life-cycle basis. Stated differently, without higher oil prices, consumers—at least initially—aren't likely to see the purchase of electric vehicles to be in their own economic interest. It is for this reason that CARB's ZEV program takes on so much importance. In the absence of politically unpopular price reforms, these regulations serve as a vital technology-forcing mechanism to bring electric vehicles into the market place.

Enhanced Support of Research and Development

Beyond pricing reform is a need to develop EV technology further. Increased shared-cost research into promising batteries, flywheels, ultracapacitors, fuel-cell designs, and hydrogen production and storage technologies would increase the odds that one or more of these technologies will become commercially viable. Without improved energy storage—higher energy densities, longer life-cycles, and lower costs—electric vehicles will remain expensive short-hop urban vehicles, useful for commuting and errands but far from all-purpose vehicles. Nickel-metal-hydride and lithium batteries are very promising, but other batteries (such as nickel-hydrogen, zinc-air and aluminum-air) and fuel cells also deserve increased support, as do the ultracapacitors and flywheels needed to help meet the high energy demands of vehicle acceleration.

Over the long term, hydrogen vehicles could surpass battery-powered EVs in two respects: longer range and shorter refueling

105

times. The keys are practicable fuel cells and on-board hydrogen storage systems. Especially in the case of hydrogen storage, DOE should fund expanded research on several of the fundamentally different approaches now in the laboratory state of development, including compressed hydrogen, liquid hydrogen, metal hydrides, cryogenic carbon adsorption, iron oxide, and liquid chemical carriers. The sooner the relative merits of these competing storage systems can be sorted out, the sooner the basic outline of a hydrogen production-and-distribution infrastructure can be sketched out.

Existing legislation already provides forward-looking support for electric vehicle development and deployment. Several titles in the Energy Policy Act of 1992 authorize EV development, including $485.3 million for battery research and development programs (1993–1998), $50 million for a decade-long EV demonstration program, $40 million for a five-year program to support research on EV infrastructure development, and $50 million to help states promote EVs. The legislation also authorizes a data-collection program, a 10-percent tax credit (not to exceed $4,000) on the purchase price of EVs, and a $2,000 tax deduction for dedicated clean fuel and flexible-fuel vehicles. Financial support for EV development is specified in other laws as well, and fully implementing these Acts would provide the support needed to accelerate EV use.

Infrastructure Development

Electric vehicles, whatever their power source, will require a widespread system of standardized recharging facilities or hydrogen pipelines, compressors, battery-recycling centers, and other equipment.[a] Normally daunting, standardizing new technologies is even harder when the status of emerging technologies is changing as rapidly as it is now. Continuing advances in on-board energy-storage devices (batteries, flywheels, ultracapacitors, hydrogen storage systems) makes early standardization per-

---

[a] The Electric Power Research Institute is supporting a major infrastructure-review effort to ensure the smooth introduction of battery-powered EVs.

ilous and potentially costly, but without agreement on storage and refueling technologies, it will be difficult to introduce these new technologies widely. Carefully designed demonstration programs, especially with fleets, could begin to dismantle these barriers, identify the most promising technologies, and help get more electric vehicles on the road.[199]

Another pressing need is for more research on systems integration and optimization—to identify the best way to put the various pieces together. Battery and hydrogen vehicles could be introduced into our transportation system in various ways, particularly if we refuel them using such renewable energy technologies as photovoltaic cells or wind machines. But where and how should these vehicles be refueled? Where and how should the energy from the renewable sources be transmitted and stored? What are the economic, safety, and reliability tradeoffs of various configurations? These questions must be answered through careful systems analysis and optimization before policy-makers can be expected to choose among the many forks in the road.

As recharging/refueling standards are adopted, building codes for residential, commercial, and industrial facilities should be modified to make new buildings "EV compatible." Initially, federal tax incentives or grants could be provided to demonstrate the use of photovoltaic arrays for EV battery-recharging at public or business parking lots.

Also needed are more trained personnel to deal with electric vehicles. Emergency professionals (fire, police, paramedics) require training to deal with accidents involving electric vehicles. On this front, Detroit Edison is already working with U.S. automakers to develop a video, manuals, and pocket guides for emergency personnel.[200] Through vocational programs, the United States should develop a service cadre for electric vehicles and, eventually, hydrogen technologies.

Stimulating Fleet Purchases

Incentives to fleet owners can stimulate the market for battery and hydrogen electric vehicles. If 10 percent of the U.S. passenger-fleet turns over each year, fleet purchases would total at least a million annually. If incentives meant that even one tenth of these vehicle were EVs—100,000 cars per year—electric vehicle manufacturers would have a robust market.

Several recent federal laws support fleet purchases. Under the Clean Air Act Amendments of 1990, some 150,000 alternative-fuel vehicles must be sold in the pilot state of California beginning in 1996 and 300,000 per year by 1999. The law also requires the introduction of alternative-fuel vehicles in other states that don't meet clean air standards. Because of the marginal benefits offered by vehicles burning methanol, ethanol, and compressed natural gas, these fleet purchase programs should focus mainly on ZEVs—battery and hydrogen fuel-cell electric vehicles.

Tax credits and deductions were established by the Energy Policy Act of 1992 for both the purchase of electric vehicles and the construction of recharging stations. In addition, the new transportation law, the Intermodal Surface Transportation Efficiency Act (ISTEA), provides unprecedented flexibility to local and regional authorities in transportation planning—in principle, affording the opportunity to integrate electric vehicles into the U.S. transportation system.

Other Measures to Get ZEVs on the Road

Many additional low-cost measures could be adopted at the state or local level to encourage the introduction of battery and hydrogen electric vehicles. States could allow electric vehicles to use HOV lanes even though they carried fewer passengers than normally required. Fees could be reduced or waived on urban toll roads. Electric vehicles could be given access to preferential parking spaces with electric recharging facilities. To reduce the long-term risk of encouraging "EV congestion," such transportation measures should have a clearly stated "sunset" provision; the preferential treatment could either expire or be phased out over a fixed period (say, ten years).

Other measures could hasten the introduction of EV-friendly infrastructure. Federal grants could be provided to municipalities that install charging meters or PV-charging arrays at publicly-owned facilities. The federal government could adopt a "Green

Car" program to showcase companies buying and using EVs in their fleets. State public utility commissions (PUCs) could permit utilities that adopt time-of-day rates for EVs to include in these rates the costs of installing ZEV-recharging equipment at homes and offices. They could also permit utilities to own and lease EV batteries to consumers—a measure that would overcome the barrier of high battery-costs and ensure battery recycling. Ford recently endorsed such a proposal.[201]

State and local vehicle fees and taxes—including annual registration fees, sales and personal-property taxes, and fuel taxes—could also be reduced or waived for a fixed introductory period, perhaps five years. Some kind of "feebate" arrangement like those designed to promote fuel-efficient cars could be used to subsidize the purchase of electric vehicles. Reduced local and state taxes, together with feebates, battery leasing, and the current federal tax credit, would go a long way toward easing the transitional problem of high first-costs faced by EV purchasers.

A remaining need is technological: standardized driving cycles should be adopted so that consumers can more accurately gauge the efficiency of electric vehicles under realistic driving conditions. Much like the federal driving cycle used for gasoline-powered vehicles, this would allow potential buyers to easily compare the relative performance (including effective range and acceleration) of various types of vehicles.

* * *

The substitution of electric cars and trucks for oil-powered vehicles will cure a major part of the nation's transportation ills. But still to be resolved are the troubles born of sprawl and congestion. For these, the answer lies in creative combinations of zoning, land-use planning, and the introduction of other emerging transportation technologies, such as personalized rapid transit.

Phasing-in battery- and hydrogen-electric vehicles would be an evolutionary leap toward a sustainable transportation system, one that will neither depend on depletable energy resources nor endanger human health or the environment. As these vehicles begin to appear in numbers, we will begin to see air pollution subside and national security improve. Once we complete the parallel introduction of renewable sources of electricity some time in the next century, we will have taken a giant stride toward protecting the earth's climate as well.

James J. MacKenzie is a senior associate in the World Resources Institute's Program in Climate, Energy, and Pollution. A physicist, Dr. MacKenzie was formerly senior staff scientist at the Union of Concerned Scientists and senior staff member for energy at the President's Council on Environmental Quality. His publications include *Driving Forces: Motor Vehicle Trends and Their Implications for Global Warming, Energy Strategies, and Transportation Planning* (WRI, 1990), *Breathing Easier: Taking Action on Climate Change, Air Pollution, and Energy Insecurity* (WRI, 1988), and, with Roger Dower and Don Chen, *The Going Rate: What It Really Costs to Drive* (WRI, 1992).

NOTES

1. National Research Council. *Rethinking the Ozone Problem in Urban and Regional Air Pollution.* Washington, D.C., 1991.
2. U.S. Environmental Protection Agency. "National Air Pollutant Emission Estimates, 1940–1990." Washington, D.C. EPA-450/4-91-026, Nov. 1991.
3. Northeast States for Coordinated Air Use Management (NESCAUM). "Adopting the California Low Emission Vehicle Program in the Northeast States, An Evaluation." Boston, Sept. 1991.
4. National Research Council. *Rethinking the Ozone Problem in Urban and Regional Air Pollution.* Washington, D.C., 1991, p. 7.
5. U.S. Environmental Protection Agency. "National Air Quality and Emissions Trends Report, 1991," Washington, D.C. 450-R-92-001, Oct. 1992, pp. 1–2.
6. Lawson, D.R. et al. "Emissions from In-use Motor Vehicles in Los Angeles: A Pilot Study of Remote Sensing and the Inspection and Maintenance Program." *J. Air Waste Manage. Assoc.* Vol. 40, No. 8, Aug. 1990.
7. U.S. Department of Energy. "National Energy Strategy, Technical Annex 2, Integrated Analysis Supporting the National Energy Strategy: Methodology, Assumptions and Results." First Edition, 1991/1992, p. 105.
8. U.S. Department of Energy, Energy Information Administration. "Annual Energy Outlook 1994." DOE/EIA-0383 (94), January 1994, pp. 121 and 143. "Monthly Energy Review." DOE/EIA-0035(93/11), Nov. 1993.
9. Georgious, G.C. "U.S. Energy Security and Policy Options for the 1990s." *Energy Policy*, Aug. 1993, pp. 831–839.

10. U.S. Department of Energy. *Annual Energy Review, 1992*. June 1993, pp. 57 and 125.
11. All data in this section are from the Department of Energy's "Monthly Energy Review," November 1993.
12. Department of Energy, Energy Information Administration. "Monthly Energy Review." November, 1993.
13. U.S. Department of Energy. "National Energy Strategy, First Edition, 1991/1992." p. 76.
14. U.S. Department of Energy. "National Energy Strategy, First Edition, 1991/1992." p. 75.
15. Intergovernmental Panel on Climate Change. "1992 IPPC Supplement, Scientific Assessment of Climate Change." 1992.
16. U.S. Environmental Protection Agency. "The Potential Effects of Global Climate Change on the United States." EPA-230-05-89-050, December 1989, p. xxx.
17. Wigley, T.M.L. and S.C.B. Raper. "Implications for Climate and Sea Level of Revised IPCC Emissions Scenarios." *Nature*, Vol. 357, May 28, 1992, p. 293.
18. Intergovernmental Panel on Climate Change. *Climate Change, the IPPC Scientific Assessment*. Cambridge University Press, 1990, page 5.
19. National Research Council. "Automotive Fuel Economy, How Far Should We Go?" National Academy Press, Washington, D.C., 1992.
20. U.S. Department of Energy, Energy Information Administration. "Annual Energy Review." 1991, DOE/EIA-0384(91), June 1992, p. 139.
21. U.S. Department of Energy, Energy Information Administration. "Annual Energy Review, 1991." DOE/EIA-0384(91), pp. 119 and 139.
22. American Automobile Manufacturers Association. "Facts and Figures '93." Detroit, pp. 18, 20.
23. Motor Vehicle Manufacturers Association. "Facts and Figures, '92." Detroit, 1992.
24. MacKenzie, James J. and Michael P. Walsh. *"Driving Forces: Motor Vehicle Trends and their Implications for Global Warming, Energy Strategies, and Transportation Planning*. World Resources Institute, Washington, D.C., 1990.

25. MacKenzie, James J. and Michael P. Walsh. *"Driving Forces: Motor Vehicle Trends and their Implications for Global Warming, Energy Strategies, and Transportation Planning.* World Resources Institute, Washington, D.C., 1990.

26. Environmental and Energy Study Conference Summary of Laws. "1990 Clean Air Act Amendments."

27. Environmental and Energy Study Institute. "Comprehensive National Energy Policy Act Conference Report, HR 776." October 1, 1992.

28. Davis, S.C. and S.G. Strang. *Transportation Energy Data Book: Edition 13.* Oak Ridge National Laboratory, ORNL-6743, March 1993, p. 3–53.

29. Boyd, James D. "California's Zero-Emission Vehicle Regulations," Proceedings of the 11th International Electric Vehicle Symposium, Florence, Italy, September, 1992.

30. American Automobile Manufacturers Association. "Facts and Figures, '93." p. 24.

31. *Electric Vehicle Progress,* November 15, 1993.

32. U.S. Congress, Office of Technology Assessment. *Replacing Gasoline, Alternative Fuels for Light-Duty Vehicles.* OTA-E-364, September 1990.

33. Gray, Charles L., and Jeffrey A. Alson. "The Case for Methanol." *Scientific American,* November 1989.

34. Sierra Research, Inc. "Ozone Benefits of Alternative Fuels: a Reevaluation Based on Actual Emissions Data and Updated Reactivity Factors," Report No. SR90-0402. Sacramento, California, April 1990.

35. Sierra Research, Inc.. "Ozone Benefits of Alternative Fuels: a Reevaluation Based on Actual Emissions Data and Updated Reactivity Factors," Report No. SR90-0402. Sacramento, California, April 1990. p.ii.

36. Personal communication with Tom Austin, January 6, 1994.

37. National Research Council. *Rethinking the Ozone Problem in Urban and Regional Air Pollution.* Washington, D.C., Dec. 1991.

38. National Research Council. *Rethinking the Ozone Problem in Urban and Regional Air Pollution.* Washington, D.C., Dec. 1991, p. 400.

39. Calvert, J.G., et al. "Achieving Acceptable Air Quality: Some Reflections on Controlling Vehicle Emissions." *Science*, Vol. 261, 2 July 1993, pp. 37–45.

40. Calvert, J.G., et al., "Achieving Acceptable Air Quality: Some Reflections on Controlling Vehicle Emissions." *Science*, Vol. 261, 2 July 1993, p. 42.

41. U.S. Congress, Office of Technology Assessment. "Replacing Gasoline, Alternative Fuels for Light-Duty Vehicles." OTA-E-364, Sept. 1990, p. 71.

42. DeLuchi, Mark A. "Emissions of Greenhouse Gases from the Use of Transportation Fuels and Electricity, Vol. 1." ANL/ESD/TM-22, Vol.1. Center for Transportation Research, Energy Systems Division, Argonne National Laboratory, Argonne, Illinois, November 1991.

43. Difiglio, C. "Methanol and Energy Security: Cost, Feedstock, and Sources of Supply," in *Methanol as an Alternative Fuel Choice: An Assessment*, edited by W.L. Kohl. School of Advanced International Studies, The Johns Hopkins University, Washington, D.C., 1990.

44. U.S. Congress, Office of Technology Assessment. "Replacing Gasoline, Alternative Fuels for Light-Duty Vehicles." OTA-E-364, Sept. 1990, p. 98; National Research Council. *Rethinking the Ozone Problem in Urban and Regional Air Pollution.* Washington, D.C., Dec. 1991, pp. 386, 388.

45. U.S. Congress, Office of Technology Assessment. "Replacing Gasoline, Alternative Fuels for Light-Duty Vehicles." OTA-E-364, Sept. 1990, p. 98; National Research Council. *Rethinking the Ozone Problem in Urban and Regional Air Pollution.* Washington, D.C., Dec. 1991, p. 402.

46. U.S. Congress, Office of Technology Assessment. "Replacing Gasoline, Alternative Fuels for Light-Duty Vehicles." OTA-E-364, Sept. 1990, p. 101; California Council for Environmental and Economic Balance. "Alternative Motor Vehicle Fuels to Improve Air Quality." San Francisco, 1990, pp. 52–53.

47. Cannon, J.S. "Paving the Way to Natural Gas Vehicles." Inform, Inc., NY, NY, 1993; U.S. Congress, Office of Technology Assessment. "Replacing Gasoline, Alternative Fuels for Light-Duty Vehicles." OTA-E-364, Sept. 1990.

48. U.S. Congress, Office of Technology Assessment. "Replacing Gasoline, Alternative Fuels for Light-Duty Vehicles." OTA-E-364, Sept. 1990, pp. 102 ff.

49. For every year between 1982 and 1992, total annual natural gas discoveries were less than annual production. Proved reserves dropped by 6 percent over this period. Source: American Gas Association. *Gas Energy Review*, November 1993.

50. Department of Energy, Energy Information Administration. "Monthly Energy Review." August 1993, p. 86.

51. U.S. Congress, Office of Technology Assessment. "Replacing Gasoline, Alternative Fuels for Light-Duty Vehicles." OTA-E-364, Sept. 1990, p. 102; *see also* Energy Information Administration. "Annual Energy Outlook 1993." DOE/EIA-0383 (93), January 1993, p. 39 ff.

52. DeLuchi, Mark A. "Emissions of Greenhouse Gases from the Use of Transportation Fuels and Electricity, Vol. 1." ANL/ESD/TM-22, Vol.1. Center for Transportation Research, Energy Systems Division, Argonne National Laboratory, Argonne, Illinois, November 1991.

53. U.S. Department of Transportation, Federal Highway Administration. "Highway Statistics, 1991." FHWA-PL-92-025, Tables MF-21 and MF-33GLA.

54. Environmental Protection Agency, Office of Mobile Sources. "Analysis of the Economic and Environmental Effects of Ethanol as an Automotive Fuel." April 1990, p. i.

55. Sierra Research, Inc. "The Air Pollution Consequences of Using Ethanol-Gasoline Blends in Ozone Non-Attainment Areas." Sacramento, California, May, 1990.

56. U.S. Congress, Office of Technology Assessment. "Replacing Gasoline, Alternative Fuels for Light-Duty Vehicles." OTA-E-364, Sept. 1990, p. 108.

57. Calvert, J.G., et al. "Achieving Acceptable Air Quality: Some Reflections on Controlling Vehicle Emissions." *Science*, Vol. 261, 2 July 1993, p. 42.

58. DeLuchi, Mark A. "Emissions of Greenhouse Gases from the Use of Transportation Fuels and Electricity, Vol. 1." ANL/ESD/TM-22, Vol.1. Center for Transportation Research, Energy Systems Division, Argonne National Laboratory, Argonne, Illinois,

Nov. 1991, p. 59.

59. DeLuchi, Mark A. "Emissions of Greenhouse Gases from the Use of Transportation Fuels and Electricity, Vol. 1." ANL/ESD/TM-22, Vol.1. Center for Transportation Research, Energy Systems Division, Argonne National Laboratory, Argonne, Illinois, November 1991, p. 120.

60. U.S. Department of Transportation, Federal Highway Administration. "Our Nation's Highways, Selected Facts and Figures," 1990, p. 31.

61. Davis, S.C. and S.G. Strang. *Transportation Energy Data Book: Edition 13*. Oak Ridge National Laboratory, ORNL-6743, 1993, p. 5–17.

62. Highway Users Federation. "Highway Fact Book, 1992," Washington, D.C., 1992, pp. 12–13.

63. Pimentel, D. "Ethanol Fuels: Energy Security, Economics, and the Environment." Cornell University, 1990.

64. U.S. Congress, Office of Technology Assessment. "Potential Environmental Impacts of Bioenergy Crop Production." Background Paper, OTA-BP-E-118, 1993, pp. 29, 33.

65. Ahmed, I. and D. Morris. "Clearing the Air About Ethanol," Carrying Capacity Network, Washington, D.C., 1992; "Meeting Transportation Needs Through Biofuels." *Energy*. Feb. 1993; Lynd, L.R. et al. "Fuel Ethanol from Cellulosic Biomass." *Science*, Vol 251, March 15, 1991, pp. 1318–1323.

66. Wyman, C.E., et al. "Ethanol and Methanol From Cellulosic Biomass," in *Renewable Energy, Sources of Fuels and Electricity*, ed. by T.B. Johansson, et al., Island Press, Washington, D.C. 1993; "Meeting Transportation Needs Through Biofuels," *Energy*, Feb.1993, pp. 23–24; Lynd, L.R. et al. "Fuel Ethanol from Cellulosic Biomass." *Science*, Vol 251, March 15, 1991, pp. 1318–1323.

67. Lynd, L.R. et al. "Fuel Ethanol from Cellulosic Biomass." *Science*, Vol 251, March 15, 1991, pp. 1318–1323.

68. U.S. Congress, Office of Technology Assessment. "Potential Environmental Impacts of Bioenergy Crop Production." Background Paper, OTA-BP-E-118, 1993, pp. 34.

69. Interlaboratory Report. "The Potential of Renewable Energy: An Interlaboratory White Paper." National Renewable Energy Laboratory, Golden, Colorado, 1990, p. B-5.

70. Interlaboratory Report. "The Potential of Renewable Energy: An Interlaboratory White Paper." National Renewable Energy Laboratory, Golden, Colorado, 1990, p. B-29, B-30.
71. Interlaboratory Report. "The Potential of Renewable Energy: An Interlaboratory White Paper." National Renewable Energy Laboratory, Golden, Colorado, 1990, p. B-6.
72. Interlaboratory Report. "The Potential of Renewable Energy: An Interlaboratory White Paper." National Renewable Energy Laboratory, Golden, Colorado, 1990, p. B-20, B21.
73. Hall, D., et al. "Biomass For Energy: Supply Prospects." in *Renewable Energy, Sources of Fuels and Electricity*. ed. by T.B. Johansson, et al., Island Press, Washington, D.C., 1993, p. 616.
74. Wyman, C.E., et al. "Ethanol and Methanol From Cellulosic Biomass." in *Renewable Energy, Sources of Fuels and Electricity*. ed. by T.B. Johansson, et al., Island Press, Washington, D.C., 1993, pp. 865–923.
75. DeLuchi, Mark A. "Emissions of Greenhouse Gases from the Use of Transportation Fuels and Electricity, Vol. 1." ANL/ESD/TM-22, Vol.1. Center for Transportation Research, Energy Systems Division, Argonne National Laboratory, Argonne, Illinois, 1991, p. 126.
76. DeLuchi, Mark A. "Emissions of Greenhouse Gases from the Use of Transportation Fuels and Electricity, Vol. 1." ANL/ESD/TM-22, Vol.1. Center for Transportation Research, Energy Systems Division, Argonne National Laboratory, Argonne, Illinois, 1991, p. 126.
77. Ogden, J.M. and M.A. DeLuchi. "Solar Hydrogen Transportation Fuels," presented at the Conference on Transportation and Global Climate Change: Long Run Options. Asilomar, CA, August, 1991; Cook, J.H., et al. "Potential Impacts of Biomass Production in the United States on Biological Diversity." *Annu. Rev. Energy Environ.*,1991, pp. 401–31; Hall, D., et al. "Biomass For Energy: Supply Prospects." *Renewable Energy, Sources of Fuels and Electricity*, ed. by T.B. Johansson, et al., Island Press, Washington, D.C., 1993; Interlaboratory Report. "The Potential of Renewable Energy: An Interlaboratory White Paper." National Renewable Energy Laboratory, Golden, Colorado, 1990.

78. Pimentel, D. and J. Krummel. "Biomass Energy and Soil Erosion: Assessment of Resource Costs." *Biomass, 14,* 1987, pp. 15–38.

79. Interlaboratory Report. "The Potential of Renewable Energy: An Interlaboratory White Paper." National Renewable Energy Laboratory, Golden, Colorado, 1990, p. 32.

80. Interlaboratory Report. "The Potential of Renewable Energy: An Interlaboratory White Paper." National Renewable Energy Laboratory, Golden, Colorado, 1990, p. 23.

81. Rosenzweig, C. and D. Hillel. 1993. "Agriculture in a Greenhouse World." *National Geographic Research and Exploration,* 9(2):208–221.

82. Rosenzweig, C, and D. Hillel. "Agriculture in a Greenhouse World." *National Geographic Research and Exploration,* 9(2):208–221, 1993.

83. DeLuchi, Mark A. "Emissions of Greenhouse Gases from the Use of Transportation Fuels and Electricity, Vol. 1." ANL/ESD/TM-22, Vol.1. Center for Transportation Research, Energy Systems Division, Argonne National Laboratory, Argonne, Illinois, 1991, pp. 63, 73.

84. Hempel, Lamont, et. al. "Curbing Air Pollution in Southern California, The Role of Electric Vehicles." Claremont Graduate School, 1989.

85. Kane, J.N. *Famous First Facts.* New York: H.W. Wilson Co., 1981, p. 53.

86. Ruddock, Ken. "Recharging an Old Idea, The Hundred-Year History of Electric Cars." *Automotive Quarterly,* Vol. 31, Number 1, 1992.

87. Ruddock, Ken. "Recharging an Old Idea, The Hundred-Year History of Electric Cars." *Automotive Quarterly,* Vol. 31, Number 1, 1992.

88. Scott, A.J., ed. "Electric Vehicle Manufacturing in Southern California: Current Developments, Future Prospects." Lewis Center for Regional Policy Studies, Univ. of California, Los Angeles, 1993, p.9.

89. Ruddock, Ken. "Recharging an Old Idea, The Hundred-Year History of Electric Cars." *Automotive Quarterly,* Vol. 31, Number 1, 1992.

90. Darling, Lloyd. "Going Jaunting in an Electric." *Popular Science*, January, 1920.
91. Ruddock, Ken. "Recharging an Old Idea, The Hundred-Year History of Electric Cars." *Automotive Quarterly*, Vol. 31, Number 1, 1992.
92. Ruddock, Ken. "Recharging an Old Idea, The Hundred-Year History of Electric Cars." *Automotive Quarterly*, Vol. 31, Number 1, 1992, pp. 30–47.
93. Hempel, Lamont, et al. "Curbing Air Pollution in Southern California, The Role of Electric Vehicles." Claremont Graduate School, 1989.
94. Harris, John A. "Good-bye Gasoline—Electric and Solar Cars are Here." January, 1991.
95. Romano, Sam. "Experience with Battery Buses as Mall Vehicles." Transpac 84, The Second International Symposium on Advanced Propulsion and Control for Urban Transit. March 4–7, 1984.
96. Personal Communications with John Capell, Executive Director, Electric Transit Vehicle Institute, Chattanooga, TN, June 29, 1993, and with Advanced Vehicle Systems, Chattanooga, TN, December 8, 1993.
97. Freedman, David H. *Discover*, March, 1992, p.90 ff; Hazleton, Lesley. "Really Cool Cars." *New York Times Magazine*, March 29, 1992.
98. Baker, Kenneth R. "The Importance of Infrastructure." Electric Vehicle Policy and Technology Conference, Los Angeles, California, March 5, 1992.
99. Frame, P. *Automotive News*, December 21, 1992.
100. Haas, Al. "General Motors Cuts Development of Electric-Powered Automobiles." Journal of Commerce, December 22, 1992.
101. Nichols, Roberta J. Testimony before the Subcommittee on Energy of the Science, Space, and Technology Committee, U.S. House of Representatives, May 11, 1993.
102. "Ford Delivers First Electric Ecostars to Utilities, UPS, DOE for Test Run." *The Solar Letter*, November 26, 1993; "Ford's Electric Vehicle Rides On a Battery Rivals Consider Too Risky," *Wall Street Journal*, December 19, 1993.

103. Sims, R.I. et al. "The Development of the Ecostar Powertrain." Proceedings of EVS-11, the 11th International Electric Vehicle Symposium, 1992.
104. "Dodge Delivers 5 Electric Vans," *Automotive News*, April 12, 1993; "Eastern U.S. Utilities Get First Chrysler TEVans," *Electric Vehicle Progress*, June 1, 1993.
105. Electric Power Research Institute. "The Chrysler Electric TEVan," 1990.
106. Samples, D.K. Testimony before the Subcommittee on Energy of the Science, Space, and Technology Committee, U.S. House of Representatives, May 11, 1993.
107. Brown, P. "Electric Vehicles Today and in the Future." Solar and Electric Vehicles, 1992.
108. Reynolds, K. "AC Propulsion CRX." *Road & Track*, October, 1992.
109. Alexander, L.A. and N. Hazard. "So You Want to Buy an EV," *Solar Age*, January/February, 1993.
110. "Firm Opens Electric Car Assembly Plant in California." *Automotive News*, April 12, 1993, p. 24.
111. "Earth Options," 1993 Catalog, Sebastopol, CA (1-800-832-1986).
112. "A Renaissance for Electric Cars." *Automotive News*, June 21, 1993.
113. Takami, T. et al. "Current Status of Electric Vehicles in Japan." EVS-11, 1992.
114. Kahlen, H. "The State of Electric Vehicles in Europe and in the World-New Technologies, Support and Coordination." Urban Electric Vehicle Symposium, May 1992, p. 56.
115. Van den Bossche, P. and G. Maggetto. "The 'Twelve Hours' Competition: A Good Way to Evaluate Electric Vehicles in City Traffic." EVS-11, September, 1992.
116. Information Bulletin. Deutsche Automobilgesellschaft mbH., November 16, 1992.
117. Press Release. "News from Volkswagen." September 7, 1992.
118. "EV Research/Testing Center Opens in La Rochelle, France." *Electric Vehicle Progress*, Vol. 14, No. 14, July 15, 1992.
119. Wolf, R. "Utility Roles in Developing and Promoting Electric Vehicles." Urban Electric Vehicle Symposium, 1992.

120. Delarue, C. "The Renault Pragmatic Approach to Cleaner European City Cars." Urban Electric Vehicle Symposium, 1992.
121. "Renault and Matra Unveil Futuristic Electric Urban Car." *Electric Vehicle Progress*, Vol.14, No.20, Oct. 15, 1992.
122. "France Pushes Forward on EV Promotion and R&D." *Electric Vehicle Progress*, Vol. 14, No.17, Sept. 1, 1992.
123. Nichols, Roberta J. Testimony before the Subcommittee on Energy, U.S. House of Representatives, May 11, 1993.
124. Nelson, R. and D. Rand. "Putting Your Best Foot Forward—A Blueprint for Lead-Acid Battery Technology and Infrastructure for Electric Vehicles." EVS-11, Florence, Italy, 1992.
125. Nelson, R.F. and D. Rand. "Putting Your Best Foot Forward—A Blueprint for a Lead-Acid Battery Technology and Infrastructure for Electric Vehicles." EVS-11, Florence, Italy, 1992.
126. Swan, D. H. "Automobiles and their Alternatives: An Agenda for the 1990's," 1990.
127. David, S.C. and M.D. Morris. 1992. "Transportation Energy Data Book: Edition 12," ORNL-6710, p. 5–6, Oak Ridge National Laboratory.
128. U.S. Advanced Battery Consortium, News Release, October 29, 1992.
129. Dowgiallo, E.J. and A.F. Burke. "Ultracapacitors for Electric and Hybrid Vehicles—A Technology Update." EVS-11, Florence, Italy, 1992.
130. Burke, A.F. "Laboratory Testing of High Energy Density Capacitors for Electric Vehicles, An Informal Report." Idaho National Engineering Laboratory, October, 1991.
131. Dowgiallo, E.J. and A.F. Burke. "Ultracapacitors for Electric and Hybrid Vehicles—A Technology Update," EVS-11, Florence, Italy, 1992.
132. Post, R.F. "Electromechanical 'Batteries' for a High-Efficiency Electric Automobile." Lawrence Livermore National Laboratory.
133. Riezenman, M.J. "The Great Battery Barrier." IEEE Spectrum, November, 1992.
134. Post, R.F. "Electromechanical 'Batteries' for a High-Efficiency Electric Automobile." Lawrence Livermore National Laboratory.

135. Post, R.F. et al. "A High Efficiency Electromechanical Battery." Lawrence Livermore National Laboratory, UCRL-JC-110861, June, 1992.

136. Lawrence Livermore National Laboratory. "Electromechanical Batteries—Energy Storage for the Future."

137. Post, R.F. "New Facts About an Old Subject: The Electric Car." Lawrence Livermore National Laboratory, November, 1990.

138. "Electric-Car Venture Adds Honeywell." *New York Times*, March 11, 1993.

139. *Electric Vehicle Progress*, June 1, 1993.

140. U.S. Department of Transportation, Federal Highway Administration. "1990 Nationwide Personal Transportation Survey, Summary of Travel Trends." PHWA-PL-92-027, March 1992, p. 18.

141. Lovins, A.B., et al. "Supercars, The Coming Light-Vehicle Revolution." Rocky Mountain Institute, Snowmass, Colorado, 1993; Bull, S.R. "U.S. Hybrid Vehicle Program." National Renewable Energy Laboratory, Presentation to Congressional Staff, Dec. 14, 1993.

142. "Transfusions Could Quickly Recharge Batteries." Automotive News, November 4, 1991.

143. Siuru, W. "Dual-Power Autos Take the Wheel." *Mechanical Engineering*, August, 1990.

144. Siuru, W. "Dual-Power Autos Take the Wheel." *Mechanical Engineering*, August, 1990.

145. Siuru, W. "Dual-Power Autos Take the Wheel." *Mechanical Engineering*, August, 1990.

146. Siuru, W. "Dual-Power Autos Take the Wheel." *Mechanical Engineering*, August, 1990.

147. U.S. Department of Energy, Office of Transportation Technologies. "Hybrid Vehicle Program Plan, Summary." November, 1992.

148. Lindquist, J., et al. "Electric Vehicle Cost Competitiveness in the United States and Europe: Implications for the U.S. Electric Vehicle Industry." EVS-10, Hong Kong, 1990.

149. MacKenzie, J., et al. *The Going Rate: What It Really Costs to Drive*. World Resources Institute, Washington, D.C., 1992.

150. Lindquist, J. et al. "Electric Vehicle Cost Competitiveness in

the United States and Europe: Implications for the U.S. Electric Vehicle Industry." EVS-10, Hong Kong, 1990.

151. DeLuchi, M. "Hydrogen Fuel Cell Vehicles." Institute of Transportation Studies, University of California, Davis, Research Report UCD-ITS-RR-92-14, Sept. 1992.

152. "Electric Dilemma." *Automotive News*, June 7, 1993.

153. Brady, J.E. and G.E. Humiston. *General Chemistry, Principles and Structure*, John Wiley and Sons, New York, 1982, p.588.

154. Ogden, J.M. and R.H. Williams. *Solar Hydrogen: Moving Beyond Fossil Fuels*. World Resources Institute, Washington, D.C., 1989, p. 31.

155. Serfass, J.A., et al. "A Practical Hydrogen Development Strategy." *International Journal of Hydrogen Energy*," Vol. 16, No. 8, 1991.

156. McLarnon, F.R. and E.J. Cairns. "Energy Storage." *Annu. Rev. Energy, 1989* 14:241–71.

157. Ogden J.M. and J. Nitsch. "Solar Hydrogen," in *Renewable Energy: Sources for Fuels and Electricity*, Island Press, Washington, D.C., 1993, Table 3. Discount rate of 6 percent is assumed. *Also*, Ogden, J. "Renewable Hydrogen Energy Systems." *Solar Today*, Sept./Oct. 1993, pp. 17–18, .

158. Ogden J.M. and M.A. DeLuchi. 1992. "Solar Hydrogen Transportation Fuels." Prepared for the Conference on Transportation and Global Climate Change: Long Run Options, Asilomar, CA. Final Draft, August 1992; Ogden, J. "Renewable Hydrogen Energy Systems." *Solar Today*, Sept./Oct. 1993, pp. 17–18.

159. Smith, D. "A National Plan for Hydrogen—A Working Document." Oct. 1991.

160. Ogden, J.M. and J. Nitsch. "Solar Hydrogen." in *Renewable Energy: Sources for Fuels and Electricity*, Island Press, Washington, D.C., 1993.

161. Johansson, T.B., et al. *Renewable Energy: Sources for Fuels and Electricity*. Island Press, Washington, D.C., 1993.

162. Ogden, J. and M. DeLuchi. "Solar Hydrogen Transportation Fuels." Conference on Transportation and Global Climate Change: Long Run Options, Asilomar, CA. Final Draft, August 1992.

163. Mayersohn, N.S. "The Outlook for Hydrogen." *Popular Science*, October, 1993.

164. Mauro, R.L. "The Technology Assessment of Hydrogen Vehicles." A Report for the National Renewable Energy Laboratory by the National Hydrogen Association, Washington, D.C., June, 1992; Ogden J.M. and J. Nitsch. "Solar Hydrogen." in *Renewable Energy: Sources for Fuels and Electricity*, Island Press, Washington, D.C., 1993.
165. U.S. Department of Energy, Office of Propulsion Systems. "Principles of Fuel Cell Operation." Nov. 1992.
166. U.S. Department of Energy. "Fundamentals of Fuel Cells." Nov. 1992.
167. Appleby, A.J. "From Sir William Grove to Today: Fuel Cells and the Future." *Journal of Power Sources*, Vol. 29, 1990.
168. DeLuchi, M.A. "Hydrogen Fuel-Cell Vehicles." Research Report, UCD-ITS-RR-92-14, Institute of Transportation Studies, University of California, Davis, Sept. 1992.
169. DeLuchi, M.A. "Hydrogen Fuel-Cell Vehicles." UCD-ITS-RR-92-14, Institute of Transportation Studies, University of California, Davis, Sept. 1992.
170. Mauro, R.L. "The Technology Assessment of Hydrogen Vehicles." A Report for the National Renewable Energy Laboratory by the National Hydrogen Association, Washington, D.C., June, 1992.
171. DeLuchi, M.A. "Hydrogen Fuel-Cell Vehicles." UCD-ITS-RR-92-14, Institute of Transportation Studies, University of California, Davis, Sept. 1992, Table 8C.
172. DeLuchi, M., et al. "Electric Vehicles: Performance, Life-Cycle Costs, Emissions, and Recharging Requirements." *Transpn. Res.-A*, Vol. 23A, No. 3, 1989, pp. 255–278; Wang, Q. et al. "Emission Impacts of Electric Vehicles." *J. Air Waste Manage. Assoc.* 40:1275–1284, 1990; Dowlatabadi, H. et al. "Electric Vehicles and the Environment: Consequences for Emissions and Air Quality in Los Angeles and U.S. Regions." Discussion Paper QE91-01, Resources for the Future, Washington, D.C., 1990; DeLuchi, M. "Emissions of Greenhouse Gases from the Use of Transportation Fuels and Electricity." Center for Transportation Research, Argonne National Laboratory, Argonne, Illinois, ANL/ESD/TM-22, Vol. 1, 1991; Gosden, D.F. "Electric Vehicles and the Greenhouse Effect." Proceedings of the 10th

International Electric Vehicle Symposium, 1990, pp. 1052–1066; Cheema, J. "Electric Vehicles and Other Clean Fuel Alternatives: A Comparative Analysis." Proceedings of the 11th International Electric Vehicle Symposium, 1992, Paper #17.01; Giugliano, M. et al. "The Contribution of Electric Vehicles to Air Quality Maintenance in Large Urban Areas." Proceedings of the 11th International Electric Vehicle Symposium, 1992, Paper #3.06.

173. DeLuchi, M. et al. "Electric Vehicles: Performance, Life-Cycle Costs, Emissions, and Recharging Requirements." *Transpn. Res.-A*, Vol. 23A, No. 3, 1989, pp. 255–278.

174. U.S. Environmental Protection Agency. "National Air Pollutant Emissions Estimates, 1940–1990." EPA-450/4-91-026, Nov. 1991.

175. Dowlatabadi, H. et al. "Electric Vehicles and the Environment: Consequences for Emissions and Air Quality in Los Angeles and U.S. Regions." Discussion Paper QE91-01, Resources for the Future, Washington, D.C., 1990.

176. Boyd, James D. "California's Zero-Emission Vehicle Regulations." Proceedings of the 11th International Electric Vehicle Symposium, Florence, Italy, Sept. 1992.

177. Northeast States for Coordinated Air Use Management (NESCAUM). "Impact of Battery-Powered Electric Vehicles on Air Quality in the Northeast States, Final Report." Boston, July, 1992.

178. U.S. Department of Transportation, Federal Highway Administration. "1990 Nationwide Personal Transportation Survey, Summary of Travel Trends." FHWA-PL-92-027, 1992, p. 8.

179. Wang, Q. and Mark DeLuchi. "Impacts of Electric Vehicles on Primary Energy Consumption and Petroleum Displacement." *Energy*, Vol. 17, No. 4, 1992, pp.351–66.

180. Electric Power Research Institute. "The Chrysler Electric TEVan," 1990.

181. Southern California Edison, Electric Transportation Division. "Electric Vehicle Efficiency Test." April, 1992.

182. U.S. Environmental Protection Agency. "Estimation of Greenhouse Gas Emissions and Sinks for the United States, 1990." Review Draft, June 21, 1993.

183. Northeast States for Coordinated Air Use Management (NESCAUM). "Impact of Battery-Powered Electric Vehicles on Air Quality in the Northeast States, Final Report." Boston, July, 1992.

184. U.S. Congress, Office of Technology Assessment. "Catching our Breath, Next Steps for Reducing Urban Ozone." OTA-O-412, July 1989, p. 17.

185. Resources For the Future. "A Fact Sheet on a 4.3 Cent Gasoline Tax Hike." News Release, July 20, 1993.

186. Ravenal, Earl C. "Defense For a New World Order." The Cato Institute, Washington, D.C., 1991, p. 46.

187. Hall, D.C. "Oil and National Security." Energy Policy, Nov. 1992.

188. DeCicco, J. and M. Ross. "An Updated Assessment of the Near-Term Potential for Improving Automotive Fuel Economy." American Council for an Energy-Efficient Economy, Nov. 1993; Ledbetter, M. and M. Ross. "Supply Curves of Conserved Energy for Automobiles." Lawrence Berkeley Laboratory, March, 1990; Koomey, J.G. et al. "Cost-Effectiveness of Fuel Economy Improvements in 1992 Honda Civic Hatchbacks." Presented at Transportation Research Board, 72nd Annual Meeting, Jan. 1993.

189. Broadman, H.G. "The Social Costs of Imported Oil," Energy Policy, Vol.14, No.3, 1986, pp. 242–252.

190. Bohi, D.R. and M.A. Toman. "Energy Security: Externalities and Policies," Energy Policy, Nov. 1993, pp. 1093–1109.

191. Spencer, D.F. "A Preliminary Assessment of Carbon Dioxide Mitigation Options." Annu. Rev. Energy Environ. Vol. 16, 1991, pp. 259–73; Synthesis Panel, Committee on Science, Engineering, and Public Policy, National Academy of Sciences, National Academy of Engineering, and Institute of Medicine. "Policy Implications of Greenhouse Warming." National Academy Press, Washington, D.C., 1991.

192. Wittenberg, Diane O. "Electric Utility Program for Development and Commercialization of Electric Vehicles." EVS-11, Nov. 1992.

193. Hester, G.L. "Electric and Magnetic Fields." Environment, Vol. 34 No. 1, Jan./Feb. 1992; Florig, H. Keith. "Containing the

Costs of the EMF Problem," *Science*, Vol. 257, July 24, 1992.

194. Coghlan, A. "Swedish Studies Pinpoint Power Line Cancer Link." *New Scientist*, October 1992, p. 4.

195. Anantaraman, A.V. et al. "A Comparative Study of Electromagnetic Fields Produced by the Operation of Electric Vehicles and Internal Combustion Engine Vehicles," EVS-11, 1992.

196. Lave, C. "Clean for a Day, California Versus the EPA's Smog Check Mandates." *Access*, University of California Transportation Center, Berkeley, CA, Fall 1993.

197. Cackette, T. "California's Zero Emission Vehicle Requirements and Implications for Hybrid Electric Vehicles," Oct. 19, 1993.

198. MacKenzie, J. et al. *The Going Rate: What It Really Costs to Drive.*" World Resources Institute, Washington, D.C., 1992.

199. Ogden, Joan M. and Robert H. Williams. *Solar Hydrogen: Moving Beyond Fossil Fuels.* World Resources Institute, Washington, D.C., 1989.

200. Moore, Taylor. "Charging Up for Electric Vehicles." *EPRI Journal*, June 1993, pp. 6–17.

201. *Electric Vehicle Progress*, November 15, 1993, p. 4.

Also from World Resources Institute...

New and recent publications on energy and transportation

A New Power Base: Renewable Energy Policies for the Nineties and Beyond
by Keith L. Kozloff and Roger C. Dower
World Resources Institute; 1993; 196 pp.; paperback
ISBN 0-915825-79-1; $24.95.

Car Trouble: Now New Technology, Clean Fuels, and Creative Thinking Can Revive the Auto Industry and Save Our Cities from Smog and Gridlock
by Steven Nadis and James J. MacKenzie
Beacon Press; 1993; 200 pp.; paperback
ISBN 0-8070-8523-5; $12.00.

The Going Rate: What It Really Costs to Drive
by James J. MacKenzie, Roger C. Dower, and Don Chen
World Resources Institute; 1992; 32 pp.; large-format paperback
ISBN 0-915825-77-5; $12.95.

To order these and other WRI publications, or to request a free WRI publications catalogue, please call 1-800-822-0503 (toll-free) or 410-516-6963, or write to: WRI Publications/P.O. Box 4852/Hampden Station/Baltimore, MD 21211. All orders must be prepaid.